I0517941

THE SHAPING OF A LIFE

ALSO BY SALLY GODDARD

Canada's Daughter: the Story of Captain Nichola Goddard

With Sister Helen Warman: *A Grand Adventure: Memoirs of a Missionary Nun*

THE SHAPING OF A LIFE

A MEMOIR

SALLY GODDARD

Copyright © 2024 by Sally Goddard

All rights reserved.

No part of this book may be reproduced in any form or by any electronic or mechanical means, including information storage and retrieval systems, without written permission from the author, except for the use of brief quotations in a book review.

Dedicated to my sisters:
Elizabeth, Alison, Hilary, and Fiona

Contents

Introduction

I have had a different kind of life than many of my peers. I can attribute that to three people.

Firstly, my father whom I felt would always rescue me should I get into trouble. This safety net that he provided, probably unconsciously, meant that no matter what decision I made, if it didn't work out, he would get me home. In reality it meant that I never second guessed myself, I just kept moving forward secure in the knowledge that he would save me. As a man who had two brothers, and was educated in private boys' schools, and then the army, his experience with women was minimal. He had five girls and common sense. That was all he needed. He made sure we were busy and encouraged us to learn as many sports and games as we could. He felt that we would fit in anywhere with those skills if we knew the rules and could play. He taught us how to play bridge and tennis, waterski, swim, skate, and ski. He encouraged us and provided the means to pursue any activity we wished. He did draw the line at certain things. He wouldn't let us toboggan—he'd seen too many head injuries. We all had to learn to drive standard—any idiot could drive an automatic. He never taught us how to drive. He said there were some skills best left to the professionals. He also had a great sense of humour but was never cruel nor vindictive with it. He loved a good story.

Secondly, my mother wanted my four sisters and I to be independent women, capable of earning a living and supporting ourselves. She encouraged us to travel and see the world. She was organized and unafraid to be different from other mothers. My father always said that she ran the house like a pediatric ward. We were expected to go to bed at a certain time, eat what was put in front of us, get up when older people came into the room, and stand at attention when *God Save the Queen* played on the radio and later on television. Everything made in England was better than things made elsewhere.

My mother supported mail order long before Amazon. Our bicycles, clothes, and toys were different from our friends. My mother didn't care and over time, we learned to cope with differences. She believed that it really didn't matter who looked after a baby, as long as it was dry and fed. As children got older, she expounded, they needed someone to be there when they got home from school, especially during their teenage years. She was so right with that one. My mother always wanted to move back to England. She felt she had only agreed to come to Canada for five years. After five years my father had a wonderful career, children whom he could do things with, a house that was big enough, and educational opportunities for his children that didn't entail boarding school. He wasn't going to go back. We grew up knowing about this longing my mother had and couldn't fulfill. It coloured everything because she wouldn't leave my father and us.

And thirdly, my husband, Tim, who always puts a pillow over his head in the mornings when I wake up and say, "I've had an idea." He has been doing this since 1977 when we married. This kind and gentle man has always supported whatever I've wanted to do. Three children later, I realized that I couldn't have it all, that someone had to be there when the girls came home from school, and available when they were sick or had unrealistic orthodontist appointments three hours drive away. Tim got the career with pensions and perks, and I got jobs, often part-time, or working from home. We would have had more money if I had taught and worked in the same school for 30 years. However, Tim would never gone back to university, and both us would have felt the strain of golden handcuffs, tying us to a place because of money rather than purpose. As we moved, I always found work, sometimes it was teaching, but more often than not it was some bizarre job that gave enormous joy and lots of stories. Tim's grandmother told him once that the gap between his teeth meant he would travel. I sometimes feel that I held onto his coattails and enjoyed the journey just as much as he has.

Sally Goddard
    Charlottetown

1. My Parents

There were two things my parents cared about as we were growing up, one was teeth and the other shoes. They always blamed the war for their poor teeth and they made sure ours were looked after. My mother felt that no one should ever have the problems with their feet that she had.

After their immigration to Canada from England in July 1952 when my older sister was 2 and I was 6 months old, my mother began tracing our feet on sheets of paper and sending them to the English relatives to buy us good shoes. This went on for years. Elizabeth, my older sister and I hated the brown leather sandals that arrived. My father eventually took pity on us and found a shoe store near his office that sold delightful leather shoes.

l-r: Sally, Alison, Elizabeth with Breck. Notice the shoes.

Their issues with teeth lasted most of their lives. I can remember coming home after a long absence and staring at my mother because she had a full set of dentures in her mouth that hadn't been there when I left. My father muddled on, losing a tooth or two every year, until he too, needed a set. He was in his 90s at this point and my sister took him to pick up his new teeth. The woman came bustling into the room with the false teeth in a container. She gave them to my father and said, "Go ahead, put them in and see what they feel like."

Try as he might, they wouldn't go in. The woman returned and said, "Just spit on them. They should just slide in." So he spat on them and got them into his mouth. According to my sister, he looked like the Cheshire cat in Alice in Wonderland. He couldn't close his lips. The woman came back in and looked and said, "I think there's been a terrible mistake. You have the wrong teeth."

⁓

My parents were both British immigrants to Canada. My father was born in 1919 in Clifftonville, the posh end of Margate, Kent. His father was a medical doctor who for a period of time was the medical superintendent of a children's TB hospital. My father was the eldest of three boys, all of whom were sent away to boarding school at the age of 7. My father began medical school in 1937 and for the first time, lived at home with his parents and took the train every day into London. At the start of the war, the medical schools in Great Britain divided the classes into two groups. One group became medics in the military and the other group was selected to complete an accelerated medical program. My father was in the second group and completed his medical training in 1942. He joined the 56th Reconnaissance Regiment after qualifying and served throughout North Africa, Sicily and Austria. After the war, he decided to specialize and do post-graduate work in internal medicine. It was at that time he met my mother at the hospital in Ilford.

My mother was born in Chesterfield, Derbyshire in 1925. My father once told me that my mother was really a country mouse. Her father was a coal miner who died of shock after escaping a mine collapse in 1952. Her mother had been a nurse in World War One, and from my understanding was a difficult woman, with a violent temper. She had my mother and her older brother and thought that she would never have more children. However, a cousin died in childbirth, and my grandmother adopted Margaret. Shortly after, at the age of 43, in 1939, she found herself pregnant with twins. At 14, my mother was babysitter and maid rolled into one. She hated the role she was expected to play. Her older brother, the apple of his mother's eye according to my mother, was not asked to help out around the house at all.

My mother had always wanted to be an actress and she felt that the war interrupted her plans. She moved to London as soon as she could to take up nurse's training at St Bartholomew's Hospital. She wanted to get away from her mother and the babies and embark on an independent life. London in the middle of the war must have been an exciting yet dangerous place. For reasons unknown, she transferred to a hospital in Ilford to complete her training. Of course, that was where she met my father who was completing his specialty training in internal medicine with an emphasis on cardiology.

They married in 1947 and spent two years in London. They moved to Grimsby where my older sister Elizabeth was born. My father then became Senior Registrar in Southport and I was born there in January 1952. By that time my father was qualified and ready to become a consultant or specialist. However, the National Health Service did not have jobs for many of the newly qualified consultants. This led my father to look elsewhere. He found a temporary job in Canada and he and my mother decided to leave England. My mother had seen newsreels where mothers and fathers had been separated from their children when they immigrated. One way around that was to travel first class. They sold what they didn't need and packed everything in three steamer trunks and boarded the Empress of Scotland on June 24, 1952 in Liverpool, landing in Montreal a week later.

2. Thessalon, Ontario
1953 - 1955

My parents first went to Kingston, Ontario for a year while my father met the requirements for the Canadian healthcare system. He worked at the clinic at Queen's University and studied for the exams he had to take.

My mother, who had qualified as a pediatric nurse before she left England, had her own ideas on parenting. Friends had given them a Millson Pram (made famous by the Royal Family) before they left England and they carefully brought it with them Everyday, rain or shine, my mother would put Elizabeth and I out in it in the front yard for an hour or two while she went back in the house. While the neighbours tolerated this in September and October, by November, they called Social Services, who paid a visit and explained the harshness of Canadian winters. She waited until spring before she put us out again.

By the spring, my father had everything in place and was offered a job in Thessalon, Ontario, between

Sudbury and Sault Ste Marie. I think a house must have come with the job as we ended up living almost next door to the Thessalon Red Cross Hospital.

My parents became involved in the Thessalon community. My mother played bridge and was active in the church. When my sister Alison was born in 1954, she was christened at the Church of the Redeemer in Thessalon. One of my earliest memories was when my father's youngest brother, Christopher, arrived from Singapore for Christmas. He took Elizabeth and I skating on the Thessalon River.

Elizabeth and Sally, Thessalon

My father was the only doctor in the area and seemed to do everything medical. A few years before he died, I drove him to my sister's cottage. We stopped in Thessalon to pick up a few things. As he and I walked slowly down Main Street, a number of people stopped and shook his hand and thanked him. He had no idea who they were or what he had done for them but I walked beside him feeling proud to be related to a man who had left a town in 1955 and who was remembered over 60 years later.

One of my father's patients was a man by the name of Bill Phillips. He had been a professional hockey player with the Montreal Maroons from 1925 until 1933. He purchased property about 15 km north of Thessalon on the Chapleau Highway and built 16 rustic cottages there. All the cottages were rentals and at one point there was a restaurant and a snack bar. He suggested to my father that it would be a good place for him to bring his family.

What started as a one week rental in 1955 went on to become a four month holiday by the 1970s. We had wonderful summers at Bill Phillips Camp. We learned how to swim and waterski, play tennis and drive a standard. Over time, my parents kept going, usually for the whole summer. My sisters and I would join them when we could but we all had summer jobs, often in different places, so visits were short.

No matter where we have lived, I have always tried to find a replacement for Bill Phillips Camp. I have never succeeded. One year, when we lived in Edmonton, we were invited to a friend's cottage for the weekend. I was so excited. When we got there it was a trailer, in a trailer park about three city blocks from the lake. The lake had leeches and worms. There was no swimming or waterskiing, no tennis, no blueberry picking. It wasn't what I expected.

On another occasion, we rented a cottage on PEI. The mosquitoes and black flies were so bad we spent a lot of time indoors. The swimming was knee-deep and rocky.

I think I will just keep my memories.

Sally, Bill Phillips Camp, 1959

3. 125 SIMPSON STREET, SAULT STE. MARIE, ONTARIO

125 Simpson Street in winter

I n 1955, my father moved the family to 125 Simpson Street in Sault Ste Marie and opened a practice in internal medicine. The house was close enough so he could walk to both hospitals. My parents lived in the same house until my mother died in December 2008. His office, for the first few years, was not particularly close to the house. Eventually, he bought into a doctors' building between the two hospitals.

I think my mother struggled to adjust to life in the Soo. She was under the impression that Canada was a 5 year stint and in 1957 or thereabouts, the family would move back to England. By September 1956, she had 4 children under the age of 6 and found things difficult. She didn't drive, my father was busy all the time, and she found the weather, especially the winters, dismal. She hired Anna R. to help her around the house. I am not quite sure why she hired a German immigrant as she hated all things German because of the war.

Many years later, I talked to Anna about her early life. Even then, she refused to tell me the name of the German town/city where she had lived. She was born in 1926 and told me that she had to join Hitler Youth in order to complete her education. When she finished school she was assigned work in a tobacco factory where she started by making cigars. Eventually, she was the office manager. The Americans arrived in their community in 1945 and her family was given one hour to move out of their house. They put everything they could into an old baby's pram and moved in with another family.

Meanwhile, Anna's future husband, Conrad, a member of the German Army, had been captured by the British after the D-Day invasion. He was sent to England to a prisoner-of-war camp where he learned English and ping pong. He returned to Germany in 1947, found work, and married Anna. He remembered stories about the German inflation after World War 1 and people having to take wheelbarrows of money to buy bread. He decided that he wanted to emigrate. Eventually, because of his English skills, he was offered a job in Ottawa.

He left on a ship as soon as a passage could be booked. He arrived in Quebec City and caught the train. He shared a compartment with a German family that were heading to a farm in a place called Echo Bay, about 20 km east of Sault Ste Marie. The wife was in tears throughout the journey. She had spent her life in big German cities and the thought of farm work in an unknown country in a remote location was driving her crazy. Coonie (as we called him) decided on that train trip to exchange papers with the man. He would go to the farm—he was used to manual labour—and the man would take his place in Ottawa. That's what they did. Apparently it took years to sort out the paperwork.

Coonie ended up on a farm belonging to a Finnish couple. It was a miserable experience and he left it as soon as he could and made his way to the Soo. He got a job at Algoma Steel, rented one room in an old house, and saved his money. He sent for Anna as soon as he had enough for a ticket to Canada. They bought a plot of land on the outskirts of the city and began building a house, adding to it as money allowed. They went to Eaton's Department Store and got the cardboard from new fridges and stoves to insulate their house. There was no running water so they carried it from a pump that was nearby. By the time Anna began working for my mother, her daughter Marion had arrived, and the house was liveable. They made Canada their home but their initial experience was somewhat different from my parents.

Anna and her husband often stayed with us when my parents went away. She was an excellent cook and explained recipes and let me work with her in the kitchen. I found I could always talk to her. She listened attentively and gave advice. After Tim and I returned to Canada, we would go and visit. They showed us how to make sausages, a skill we took to Northern Canada.

Anna continued to visit my mother long after she finished working for her. I think she was checking up on her. They were both immigrants, from different backgrounds, but with similar bouts of homesickness and a longing for a life that wasn't going to happen.

Over time everyone settled into life on Simpson Street. My father was busy establishing himself and his practice. My mother found friends who showed her the ropes. Our first school was at the top of the street so we walked or rode our bikes. My mother didn't drive until 1966 and my father was usually not available so we learned how to use the bus and joined activities like Brownies and Girl Guides to which we could walk or bike. My father introduced us to skiing—he had learned when he was in Austria during the war. For a number of years, he would take my sisters and me to the local ski hill on Saturday mornings, give us each $1–50 cents for the tow and 50 cents for lunch—and would return to work. He would join us in the afternoon. On Sundays, he would take us to the bigger ski resorts in the area. My mother never joined us. She would relish having the day to herself and always had a wonderful meal ready for us on our return. In the summer, we would be at the cottage, swimming, waterskiing, blueberry picking, and playing games. There was no television and my parents would encourage us to go outside, no matter what the weather.

My mother, especially, loved Christmas. The build-up started around Thanksgiving when my mother retrieved an old baby's bath from the basement and used it to mix the Christmas puddings. This was followed by the baking and eventual icing of the Christmas Cake. Then, she made mincemeat pies. When presents were purchased, they were stored under my parents' bed. My mother directed the Nativity play at church and practices were every Sunday afternoon starting after Remembrance Day. The performance was always wonderful and really started Christmas.

The angels at the nativity pageant: Jane Wadley (l),
Sally (r) The Sault Star, 22 December 1958

She would book phone calls to England as there was no direct dialling. We were expected to be home on the afternoon of Christmas Eve to wish Merry Christmas to relatives we barely knew. After supper on Christmas Eve, she would read us the story of that first Christmas and we were expected to go to bed after hanging up our stockings. On Christmas morning, we would go to church, return for breakfast, and then line up by age from the youngest to the oldest, before the door to the living room was opened and Christmas really began.

Sally and Elizabeth: Christmas 1957

For a number of years, my father would take us over to the General Hospital to visit with the nuns while my mother got Christmas lunch organized. Years after we had all left home, my father was visiting the nuns at Christmas. Sister Teresa Agatha and Sister Marguerite asked after us girls. He reported on Elizabeth, Alison, Hilary, and Fiona and his final comment was "and Sally has gone off and married some guy in the jungle."

My mother also joined the Sault Theatre Workshop in the late 1950s and 1960s. She performed in many of their productions at the time.

In 1963, Mum directed and was the leading actor in *Epitaph for George Dilon*. The adjudicator remarked that "Kathy West's acting is enough to consider her for best actress. She has sense and intelligence" (*Sault Star*, April 1, 1963). She was also commended for portrayal of Helen Keller's mother in *The Miracle Worker*. The adjudicator, Mme. Beaubien, said "Kathleen West as Kate Keller made us feel all the emotions that a mother in her position can feel. She never overdid it. Her movements were graceful and right and she knew how to walk in a long gown" (*Sault Star*, May 2, 1966).

There was a constant procession of real actors and want-to-be actors through the house. We would hear the party going on but never dreamt of going downstairs. In the morning we would often wake people up who had slept over or passed out, depending who was explaining their presence to us.

I don't think I was aware of how good an actress she was. By the time I was a teenager, she had left the Sault Theatre Workshop and was working with the Cathedral Players as part of St. Luke's Cathedral, the church she and my father attended. She directed *Christ in the Concrete City* by Phillip Turner, and acted as Alice More, the wife of Sir Thomas More, in *A Man for All Seasons* in 1973.

One evening, an old acting friend of my mother's showed up, needing a place to stay. Alison was moved out of her room into Hilary's and this woman was given Alison's room. My youngest sister Fiona, who must have been 6 or 7 at the time, periodically crawled into bed with Alison when she had a bad dream. She was already asleep when this woman arrived so didn't know that Alison wasn't there. Fiona tiptoed down the hall, opened the bedroom door, and crawled into bed. It was only when this woman rolled over, that Fiona realized it wasn't Alison. She never did it again.

Long before we became teenagers, my mother became a beacon for girls in trouble. There were several unwed mothers whom my mother helped find homes and supported as they made decisions about their babies. She urged the babysitter we had to go to university and become a teacher. She advised on wedding dresses. I remember her telling one bride whose wedding dress was extremely short, "It doesn't matter now but in 50 years time what are your children going to think?" Our friends wanted to come to our house just to look at my mother because to them she was a beatnik, part of the new generation. She was never a housewife in the traditional sense.

I doubt that my mother realized it at the time, but she provided us with examples of sharing and hospitality that I like to think I have tried to emulate throughout my life. She also never conformed, never tried to fit in. She was who she was. Of course, as a child and a teenager, it didn't help, but she taught me to be myself. There was nothing wrong with not conforming.

They also exhibited different parenting strategies than our friends' parents. They never grounded us because my mother felt that it punished the parents more that the children. We were always given an allowance, not based on the chores we did, but based on our ages. The jobs we did around the house we were expected to do, not because we were paid. One of my sisters wanted my parents to buy a piano because all her friends were taking piano lessons. My father never said no outright. He made arrangements for her to take lessons from the nuns in the convent at the top of our street. The nuns would also let her practice every day after school. My father told her that if she kept it up for three months he would buy her the piano she desperately wanted. She quit three weeks later and there was never a mention of the piano again.

My father rented a motor boat at the cottage every year and every year, we would beg him to let us drive it.

He said when we could start it, we could drive it. The cord you had to pull was tricky and not easy. He said that if we were out in the lake on our own, we had to be able to start it. It took me three years before I could do it. When we were old enough to drive, he insisted that we learned to drive a standard. "Any idiot can drive an automatic," he was fond of saying.

My father felt that we all needed a 'ticket', some way of making a living. It didn't matter what we did as long as we could support ourselves. My mother insisted that we experience life outside of the Soo. It was important, she felt, that we saw as much as we could of the world round us and encouraged travel.

In 1963, my parents took four of us to England and France. They left our youngest sister who was 18 months old at the time with family friends. My mother felt that Fiona would not remember anything and was still in diapers—disposable ones had not been invented. Of course she was right. Fiona wouldn't have remembered anything. I often think of that when I see people taking their toddlers on the plane to Disneyland. How much will they remember? Who is the trip for?

My father decided to rent a Bedford dormobile camper van while we were there. It slept 4 but the man he rented it from threw in a tent and two sleeping bags so it could sleep 6. The original plan was for the 4 girls to sleep in the dormobile and my parents to sleep in the tent. The tent was never used.

The four of us found ourselves sleeping in the van in people's driveways and hotel parking lots. My parents enjoyed visiting their friends and families and staying in their guest rooms. When we went to France, my mother always found a hotel with a large parking lot. On our last day in London, my parents gave each of us £1 and let us loose in Hambly's Toy Store for one hour. At that time it was the largest toy store in the world. I can still remember that I bought a set of mechanical coloured pencils that were different from any I'd ever seen.

In 1966, high schools began offering chaperoned trips to Europe. I went on the first one and had a fabulous time on a two week bus tour of Europe followed by a week cruising on the Mediterranean. My older sister did the same trip the next year. One of the participants bought a bicycle in Europe and took it apart. Each person on the trip was given a piece to bring back. The fellow got all the pieces at the airport and put the bike together.

Fares to England were cheap and all of us benefitted from visiting England specifically. Another sister flew to Scotland with a friend. Her friend's parents had made arrangements for distant relatives to pick them up from the airport and look after them for a few days. As the girls came into the arrivals level, they were swept up by an enthusiastic couple with heavy Scottish accents. They got their luggage in the car and started driving. The woman asked a number of questions about people that they knew in Canada. It slowly dawned on the girls that they were with the wrong couple. They were immediately taken back to the airport and dropped off. The right girls were waiting patiently, if not somewhat confused when my sister and her friend got out of the car.

It seemed like almost everybody went to Expo '67. My

father rented a cottage for a week in St Jean, just outside of Montreal. Every day, we would drive into the city and take the Metro to the Ile de Montreal. We each had our own Expo '67 passport and wandered in small family groups, taking it all in. My mother discovered the Jamaican pavilion, and no day was complete without her having one or two Yellow-bird Whistles, Jamaican rum inspired drinks, before leaving the island. My father always drove and my mother navigated. The five of us were in the back. There were no seat belts. We never went back to the cottage the same way. My mother's map reading skills matched my father's driving abilities. One memorable evening we ended up at the United States border crossing.

We did have a lovely time and when we loaded the car to go home, my mother's suitcase had to go on the roof rack because there was no room inside the car. When we arrived in the Soo, my mother organized the emptying of the car, and then supervised the emptying of the suitcases. The doorbell rang, and my mother answered it. There were two policemen there. They asked her if she had lost anything. My mother said she didn't think so. Then one of the policeman produced her suitcase which had flown off the roof on the outskirts of the Soo. They had dug through her dirty clothes and eventually found her Expo '67 passport.

All of us went away to church camps and Girl Guide camps, which usually lasted about a week.

Elizabeth (left) and Sally (right) waiting for the bus to take them to the Girl Guide Camp at Doe Lake

One of the curates from the church had been to see my father on a health related issue. He mentioned that he was trying to get enough teenagers to go with him for a canoe camp with some older students from the Shingwauk Residential School.* My father immediately signed me up. I was 14 or 15 and he thought I needed something to do. I couldn't argue with him and on the assigned date, he drove me to the Ontario Provincial Police station on Hwy 17 East and we waited for the bus to stop and pick me up. You could see it coming from quite a distance as the old school bus belonging to the Shingwauk Residential School belched black smoke as it trundled down the highway at about 30 mph. I just hoped no one saw me get on the bus. The doors opened, my father threw in my knapsack and my sleeping bag, said goodbye and left me. The curate was driving the bus and told me to find a seat. Almost every seat was full of male students from the residential school. I sat by myself, behind the curate, silently cursing my father. It was going to be a long 10 days. No one on the bus was speaking English, they were on holiday and speaking their home language. I felt very alone.

We eventually turned at Espanola and made our way to Camp Manitou, a summer camp run by the Algoma Diocese of the Anglican Church of Canada. It turned out that the daughter of the camp cook was coming as well and we ended up sharing a tent. The next day we began the canoe trip and I can't tell you how much I enjoyed it. Language and cultural barriers vanished and when my father picked me up 10 days later, I was not sitting on my own. In fact, the trip back was like a cocktail party, as I visited everyone before saying goodbye.

The next summer, I applied and was accepted to spend six weeks helping to run a summer camp in a place called Harrington Harbour, an island in the Gulf of St Lawrence, just north east of Anticosti Island. I had heard about the job the year before from a friend of my parents who had travelled there as a young man to work with Dr. Grenfell. I had read about Dr. Grenfell in one of our readers at school. He was a medical doctor who served the needs of the people living on the Lower North Shore of the St. Lawrence River as well as the Labrador Coast and parts of Newfoundland. He set up a series of nursing stations and staffed them with British nurses who tended to stay and marry into the community. He ran a dog team so he could travel between communities in the winter. At one point, so the story goes, the ice he was travelling on broke away and he and his dogs were trapped. He ended up having to eat a couple of his dogs in order to survive.

Dr. Grenfell died in 1940 but his influence was still strong when I first went to the coast in 1970. I was part of a group of volunteers under the auspices of the Quebec Labrador Foundation and its founder, Rev. Bob Bryan. Bob flew a seaplane between communities, conducting church services including baptisms, marriages, and funerals. He also visited the volunteers running the day camps for the children of the communities. Our job was to keep the children occupied while their parents worked. In those days, the men fished for cod in the summer and hunted seal in the winter. The women would help the men preparing the cod for market. School was finished for the summer so we became the entertainment.

I flew to Sept Iles and met the other volunteers. We all boarded the Fort Mingan, the freighter that travelled between Sept Iles and Blanc Sabon weekly with supplies and passengers. There were shared cabins and an eating area for our meals. Each time the ship stopped, a couple of the volunteers got off and blended into the crowd, not to be seen or heard from for six weeks; the freight would be offloaded, and the ship continued to the next stop. I remember seeing an iceberg for the first time and thinking that I hoped the captain knew that two-thirds of the ice was under the water.

Eventually, I got off with two other volunteers at Harrington Harbour and began one of the most treasured experiences I have ever had. The other female volunteer and I were taken to Maud Bobbit's house. There were no cars in the community but there were boardwalks that connected houses and community buildings. Everyone's house had a long hose with many attachments that ran from the reservoir at the top of the hill behind the village to each person's house. The water ran into large barrels kept on everyone's porch. If the water wasn't running, someone had to follow the hose to see where it had come apart and reattach it.

Aunt Maud, as we called her, was close to 80 then, and we had a wonderful time with her, learning the ins and outs of living in a house that didn't have a television but a radio, and had a telephone that was private and long distance calls were prohibited because they we so expensive. She had lived in Harrington Harbour her entire life. The stove was always on and there was always tea in the pot. At one point she took the teapot off the stove and the bottom came away. I shared a bedroom with a girl from New York. She had a grant from the Polaroid Foundation and had brought a number of Polaroids and film with her. She encouraged the students to take pictures by theme —someone you love, someone you admire—and then had them explain why. Over the summer she collected a number of them and sent a display to Polaroid at the end of the summer.

I didn't have anything special to offer. I had worked with kids in Brownies and Girl Guides. I could organize arts and crafts, play baseball and teach the younger ones to play 'Duck, Duck, Goose.'

Summer 1970: Sally on a fishing boat near Harrington Harbour

I picked berries, collected shells, and provided materials for any artistic creations. We were invited to community events and joined the rest of the community at the wharf whenever the Fort Mingan arrived.

In those days, people still kept dogs to pull their sleds. Although Skidoos (snowmobiles) had been invented, they were expensive for the average person who fished for a living. Everyone's dogs were pegged out away from the houses. They were fed just enough to stay alive. Once they started working, they were fed more. One of the three year olds who had been at the day camp, got too close to her father's dogs and was killed. Bob Bryan flew in for the funeral. It was the first one I ever attended. Her brothers carried this little white coffin in and out of the church. It was one of the saddest things I have ever experienced.

We kept going because that was what was expected. The summer ended and we were taken by fishing boat to Chevery, the closest community with an airport and flown to Sept Iles where we said an emotional goodbye to each other and returned home.

I returned two years later, as a day camp councillor at Mutton Bay (Baie de Mouton) for six weeks. It was further up the coast on the Fort Mingan route. The families continued to follow the seasonal way of life. They fished for cod in the summer and hunted seal in the winter. At that time, when children finished Grade 8 at the community school, they had to leave and attend secondary school and later CJEP in Sherbrooke in Quebec's Eastern Townships where they would be billeted with families. They would return home for Christmas and summer holidays. Many didn't last, didn't see the purpose of further education if they were going to follow in their parents' footsteps and be fishers and sealers. Often, the adjustment was too hard and they left early. They didn't think that they needed more education.

Into this I stepped as a day camp councillor. I was billeted with Lexi, an American from Washington, DC. We lived with a couple and their three young girls for the summer. We talked about the future for their children. They knew that the hunting and fishing lifestyle was not going to last forever. They were afraid to encourage their children to go and afraid what would happen to them if they didn't go. I think that was when I had an idea. I would take students from Grades 6-8 across Canada so they could see what was available to them.

It took us two years to raise the money. I asked a friend of mine, Nancy Moore, to help. Her dad, Jake Moore, suggested corporations and individuals who might be interested. Nancy wrote begging letters to all of them as well as filling out funding applications. Bob Bryan and the QLF (Quebec Labrador Foundation) provided tax receipts. Archbishop W. L. Wright, the Archbishop of Algoma at the time, lived across the street from my parents. At a cocktail party, I talked to him about the project. He took a keen interest and after I gave him a rough itinerary, he contacted an Anglican church at each location. He suggested they help us by providing a place for 32 students and 6 councillors to sleep and eat. He also managed to get us a grant from the Anglican Foundation for $2000. Between government grants, private donations and connections, we raised enough, and the trip was set for July 1974.

Called Linking Canada Coast to Coast, we went by bus to Vancouver and flew back. I returned once again on the Fort Mingan to pick up 32 students, 11-14 years old, from the small communities along the Lower North Shore of the St. Lawrence. On the first day, the bus picked us up and we started driving down the highway. The kids were intrigued by the white lines on the road and the signs that said 60. There were no paved roads in their communities at that time and no television. The bus driver patiently explained what the different traffic symbols meant. We often found the boys sitting behind the driver, reminding him when he was exceeding the speed limit and when he went over the lines.

I was 22 when I went to pick up the students. Using today's standards, nobody in their right mind should have let their children go with us. Recently, I had the opportunity to talk to a few of those who came on that trip. Their parents, it seems, had been the ones eager for their children to see Canada. They were excited at the prospect of the trip but for some, there were lasting repercussions. They learned what Canada was. They saw poor people on the streets, they met people whose generosity knew no end. Some learned to swim, some saw jobs they wanted to do. They all encouraged their own children to explore whenever an opportunity presented itself. The trip made them less afraid of the outside world.

We slept in church halls, sometimes with food. Often, we all prepared supper and then made lunches for the next day. It was a hot summer and we tried to find swimming pools in each place we stopped. Few of the children could swim but luckily, one of the councillors had been a swimming instructor in a previous life, and many of the children learned to swim. We flew the children back and I had to leave the group in Toronto to return to Sault Ste Marie as I was heading to Papua New Guinea in a few days' time.

Oddly enough, when we lived in Calgary, we went to see a movie called *Seducing Dr. Lewis*. As the movie went on, I became more and more convinced that I had been where it was filmed. As the credits came on at the end, it showed that it was filmed in Harrington Harbour, a place I hadn't been back to since the mid-1970s.

Many years later I attended Bob's 80th birthday celebration in the Eastern Townships. There was a man playing a squeeze box who looked vaguely familiar. He was outside having a smoke and I explained who I was. He said he had been on the 'Linking Canada Coast to Coast' trip. He looked up at me, smiled at me and said, "Some fun that was."

I finished my Grade 12 in Sault Ste. Marie and then completed Grade 13 in Lausanne, Switzerland. It was a totally self-indulgent year, and I can only echo that boy who came across Canada with us by bus and say, "Some fun that was!" Upon my return to Canada, there were two pieces of mail. The first was my acceptance to Trent University as well as a place in residence and secondly, a letter was from a fellow that I had met who had chosen to go to the Royal Military College in Kingston, Ontario. In those days, new recruits had to be clean shaven, so wrapped up in his letter inviting me to the Christmas Ball, was his beard. It's not often I am at a loss for words but this was one of those times. Beard hair is not attractive separated from a face but in a way it was a romantic gesture. I accepted the invitation to the ball and invited him home for Christmas.

Luckily, I had a ball gown. A few years before, an acquaintance of my mother phoned and asked if I would go with her son to a military ball at the Armouries in Sault Ste Marie. Of course my mother was thrilled, and if memory serves me correctly, accepted on my behalf. It was not something I wanted to do but my mother was the master of guilt using sentences like, "I would have loved to have gone to a dance like that but there was a war on," and "My mother needed me to look after the twins all the time." I got sucked into that vortex. I had never met the guy. My mother organized the ball gown—numerous fittings—and to my chagrin, dance lessons with the next-door neighbour. I had a list of topics to talk about put together by my sisters.

The fellow couldn't drive so his father drove him to our house. He was wearing his sea cadet uniform. I am sure his mother had pressed it but by the time he arrived at our house, he looked like he'd slept in it. I was presented with a corsage to wear on my wrist and we drove over to his house for pictures. I hope to God there is no evidence of that evening. We got to the dance early. He knew no one and he gave one-word answers to any question I asked. By 9 o'clock I had exhausted all the topics on my list. It was excruciating. When the music finally started, the dancing involved shuffling round the room, clinging on to each other, regardless of whether the music was fast or slow. Eventually, his father showed up to take us home. I never saw nor heard from him again.

I took my ball gown with me to Trent. When Christmas rolled around I took the bus to Kingston where an old friend from the Soo was in residence at Queen's and she let me use her room to change. I entered the room where the dance was held and was almost overcome by the sea of red uniforms. It was like something out of a film set in colonial Africa, with all the British soldiers wearing red serge uniforms to hide the blood if they were shot. At the end of the evening, we got the bus to Toronto, arriving there just as it was getting light. We surprised my friend's grandmother but she gave us breakfast. We flew to the Soo and I spent my holidays, selfishly, realizing that my feelings for the soldier had disappeared. He, on the other hand, wanted something more permanent and that just wasn't going to happen. He left RMC before the end of his first year. The last time I saw him was in 1976 when he and his wife had just had a baby.

Because Ontario schools went to Grade 13 at the time, university degrees were completed in three years. I spent two years in residence and the third year living with a group in an apartment. I got involved in student government, rowed and skied for the university, and gradually became a better student. At the end of my second year, I flew to Whitehorse in the Yukon with a friend. She had heard that it was easy to make money. We shared a room at a residential hotel and got waitressing jobs almost immediately, and were paid minimum wage plus tips. We were just breaking even after a couple of weeks when my friend heard of waitressing jobs in Dawson City, a 6 hour car ride away on the Klondike Highway.

We got the jobs which included housing and found ourselves in the back seat of a car with the cook and the manager of the new restaurant, driving north. Our new employers had a case of 24 beers between them in the front seat and drove and drank, occasionally throwing a beer bottle out the window. We were glad to get to Dawson in one piece and found that we were sharing subsidized housing with our employers. There were two single mattresses on the floor for us and we all used the same bathroom. As it turned out, the work was great, the pay was good, and the tips were generous. Our bosses knew what they were doing. By the end of the summer we had enough money to fly out of Dawson to Whitehorse and back to Ontario.

During my last year at Trent, I struggled to figure out what I was going to do when I graduated. I had spent a couple of weeks in a law office as a Girl Friday and I thought law might be a good career. Without any preparation, I decided to take the Law School Admission Test (LSAT) in the fall. I was so totally humiliated by the experience, I never applied for law school.

That year, one of my classes was held across the hall from the career office. I happened to see a poster advertising Canadian University Service Overseas (CUSO). The organization was looking for new graduates to work in a variety of occupations and countries. There was a two year commitment; return airfare, housing, and medical support was provided by CUSO. The government of the host country paid the volunteer's salary, which would be the same as what a national from that country would earn in the same job.

My parents were supportive of the CUSO experience. My father equated it to the time he spent in the army. He also appreciated the fact that it wouldn't cost him anything. My mother thought the experience would be wonderful. She wasn't quite sure where I was until a *National Geographic* magazine had a story and a map on Papua New Guinea.

I applied, was accepted, and was eventually posted to Papua New Guinea to teach at Cameron High School in Alotau, Milne Bay Province. There was an orientation at the University of British Columbia in Vancouver—the same week I was there with the students on the bus trip. I was able to spend an evening with the group going to Papua New Guinea.

Once the bus trip was over, I began the long journey to Australia, on the same day American President Nixon resigned. When the pilot announced it the whole plane cheered.

As part of the orientation material I was given a booklet written by CUSO for volunteers going to PNG. One of the articles was titled 'Missionaries, Mercenaries, and Misfits', which described the people that tended to work in Papua New Guinea from overseas. The only category I fit in was 'misfit', and I wondered how true that was.

The CUSO field manager met me at Jackson Airport in Port Moresby, the capital city of Papua New Guinea. In those days (August 1974) it took a while to get through customs as they had to check and make sure you didn't have any playing cards or babies' bottles. Both were banned. The former because of gambling and the latter because of hygiene issues. I was taken to the Civic Guest House in Boroko where I met other volunteers who were waiting for flights to their postings. I shared a room with another girl who was heading in the same general direction as myself. I soon realized that I needed a pair of flipflops or sandals. Both my running shoes and my lovely Roots leather shoes were too hot. I took one look at what my roommate had on her feet and suggested she get a pair as well. She said she wasn't going to get a pair and proceeded to take off her right shoe and sock. She only had a big toe. All the other toes had been lost to a lawn-mower accident when she was 2 years old.

4. CAMERON HIGH SCHOOL, ALOTAU: 1974-1979

After a couple of days in Port Moresby, the capital of Papua New Guinea, I flew to Alotau, the provincial capital of Milne Bay Province, to teach English and Social Studies at Cameron High School.

I was given a two-bedroom furnished house in the school compound. It had a fridge and a wood stove that also heated the hot water. Once the stove was lit, it had to burn for an hour or two before there was any hot water, which then lasted for about a day. It wasn't practical or necessary to light the stove in the morning. I bought an electric jug to boil water and a kerosene burner so I could cook without lighting the stove.

I had never lived on my own before. The food was different. I could buy fresh vegetables at the market but I didn't know what to do with many of them—bush greens, ibika, mango, pawpaw, plantains were all foreign to me. There were three trade stores in Alotau. They stocked frozen food from Australia and tinned food from around the world. Butter came in tins from Denmark. Whole chickens were in tines the size of large tomato juice cans. When you opened the tin, the chicken came sliding out covered in jelly. Once released, its wings and legs sprang open.

The students paid school fees. It wasn't a lot but if your parents were subsistence farmers or fishermen, it was often difficult to get the money. Some students arrived and found work with teachers on the weekends, cutting wood for the stoves, doing dishes, washing clothes, to pay their fees.

The students cooked for themselves. The food was provided, mainly tinned fish and brown rice three times a day. The boys got the wood for the fires that cooked the rice. The tinned fish was mixed with bush greens when possible. Every now and again, one of the school cows was butchered. The teachers cut up the cow and the meat was given to the mess. I learned how to butcher a cow, a skill that came in handy when we later lived up north. The meat was stored in a walk-in freezer close to the mess.

For some reason, there were multiple copies of *Call of the Wild* in simplified English in the English classroom. I began reading it with the Grade 8 students, and soon realized they had no idea what cold was. I took them down to the walk-in freezer and had them go inside. No one wore shoes and just had t-shirts and skirts or shorts. It was quite the learning experience.

I soon adapted to the life of a teacher at a boarding school. I taught from 7:00 am until 1:00 pm, with a 30 minute recess in the middle. Lunch was from 1:00 pm–

2:00 pm. From 2:00 pm–4:00 pm, all the teachers supervised work parade three afternoons a week. The students had jobs to do around the school that included grass cutting, cleaning, washing and cooking. One afternoon was for sports and one afternoon was for clubs. I started a Girl Guide group that was reasonably popular. At one point, one girl was selected for an international camp in Australia.

I did have a few miss-steps. On one occasion, I found some light coloured uniforms that no one was using and I thought if I dyed them navy blue, the girls could wear them as Girl Guide uniforms. I dyed the dresses but did not know that I had to fix the dye. The girls wore them in a parade and when it started to rain, the navy blue dye ran down their legs. They never complained.

On another occasion, I decided that I would do a navity play with the students, modelling it after my mother's rendition. We used straw in the manager and lit the stage with kerosene lamps. Luckily, one of the other teachers stomped the fire out before it took hold.

I spent my first Christmas at the school. I taught a Grade 8 Adult Education class with Brother McCann, a longtime Catholic teacher. He was such a good teacher that at one point I suggested that we switch classes so that my students could have the benefit of his skill. He told me that I was doing just fine, that the students were enjoying my class and that was all that mattered. I don't remember missing Christmas very much.

There was a certain amount of supervision that was shared among staff. When you were on duty, it was 24/7 for a week. You had to make sure the girls were up to cook breakfast, that everyone got to breakfast, that the mess area was cleaned after each meal, that the students went to night study from 7:00 pm–8:30 pm and the lights went out at 9:00 pm. I think we did duty three or four times a year.

There was an international group of teachers at Cameron. There were Australian, English, Phillipino, Canadian volunteers, and local teachers. All staff lived on site and each nationality was paid at a different level. The Australians made the most, followed by the English and then the Phillipinos. The volunteers were paid at the same rate as the local teachers. Some people found it difficult to rationalize the pay difference but it never really bothered me. I had a house to live in, and enough money to buy what I needed.

The first eighteen months I lived in Papua New Guinea, I didn't have any transport. I had to rely on friends, passing vehicles, and my feet. I didn't miss the cars and buses of North America too much, though there were days when I would have loved to have been behind the wheel of my father's V8 station wagon and taken off. The boarding school life absorbed me and there was a small canteen where you could buy bits and pieces. I never had much money, so there was no point in racing off to town.

Alotau, 1975

The main road followed the coastline joining Alotau to the airport and to the Catholic mission station at Hagita. It was about 15 km to the airport from the school; three km to the four stores; four km to the church, and about five km to the hospital. If I needed to go to town I would walk and more likely than not someone would stop and give me a ride.

In November 1975, the Department of Education discovered that they had made a mistake with my pay and awarded me 18 months back pay. Needless to say, it was a substantial amount. I was able to purchase a green Honda 70 motorbike from a departing Australian teacher, complete with a shocking pink helmet. It was more like a scooter. There was no clutch to change and there was a wide flap from the handlebars to the footrest so that wearing a dress and driving a motorbike did not present a problem. I went out to Hagita several times, getting to know Sister Helen Warman and Sister Margaret Jennings as well as the volunteers that taught in the mission school.

Another teacher and I went to New Zealand for my second Christmas away. We were gone for about a month and I was glad to get back to Alotau for my final eight months.

A group of British teachers had been hired and flown to Port Moresby. Three of them were assigned to my school. Arty and Jenny Morson came with their two children fresh from a difficult time in Uganda under Idi Amin. Tim Goddard, the third, was a relatively new graduate who had taught for a year in Harlow, a working-class 'new town' just north of London, before coming to PNG. I met him when the power lines came down near my house. I suggested that he not jump them as they could still be live. In my memory, I thought he was going to. In his, he was just looking and wouldn't do anything that stupid.

There weren't many single men in Alotau. Rob VanDerLoos, a local entrepreneur, was engaged. Other teachers did not appeal. Tim was his own man. The Australians on staff wore regular shorts that came halfway down their thighs. Tim wore Bombay bloomers, white Navy shorts with wide legs, that he had picked up second hand at an Army surplus store in London. Eventually, Tim modified his wardrobe, but he certainly didn't care what others thought.

He was a superb teacher, full of ideas and enthusiasm. He had been hired as a Manual Arts teacher, even though he had trained in Expressive Arts and Geography. It didn't bother him that he knew nothing about building furniture. He learned with the students. The school let him teach a few Expressive Arts classes as well.

Tim purchased a red Honda 70 motorbike from a departing teacher. One Saturday afternoon, I had an idea. I went round to Tim's house to see if he could be coerced into a motorbike ride. It had rained all morning but the sun had begun to shine. I asked him, "Do you want to go out to the airstrip and watch the plane come in?" As the plane only landed once on Saturday, the little tea shack beside the terminal building would be open. "We could have a cup of tea, see who gets off the plane and then come home," I said enticingly.

Tim was not convinced. "It's so wet. Do you think the plane will even land? I don't want to get all the way out there to find nothing."

We started off. About two km out of town was a gravel creek that was fed by the interior mountains. It was not very deep and Tim led us across. We were surprised that it was not deeper after all the morning rain.

The plane had not arrived by the time we got to the airstrip. We had a cup of tea and were just about ready to give up seeing the plane from Port Moresby, when a truck rolled up and a pilot we knew got out. "Hey you two, I have to go pick up a medical emergency on the islands. A guy has fallen between the wharf and a boat that was tied up. He broke his leg. I have room for one passenger. Do one of you want to come?" There was a small plane parked at the airstrip that he was going to take.

Tim was excited—this was an adventure, flying in a small plane to pick up a medical emergency. I'd been in Alotau longer than Tim. The thought of bouncing around in a small plane for hours was something I could miss. "You go. I went there last year. Don't worry about me. I'll go to the Catholic mission at Hagita, visit the two British volunteers who are teaching there and meet you back at the airstrip."

The pilot said he'd be back by 5:00pm. I watched Tim clamber into the front seat of the plane, put on the earphones, and wave. They were gone. I got back on my bike and went to Hagita to visit my friends. Virginia, a British volunteer, had not been in the country for very long and decided that she really wanted to see the hotspots of Alotau. I suggested that she ride on the back of my motorcycle to the airstrip. We would meet Tim and travel together back to town.

We got to the airstrip just after 5:00 and there was no sign of anyone. At about 5:45 I was beginning to get worried as it would be dark just after 6:00. The airstrip did not have landing lights and planes were not allowed to fly after dark. Suddenly, there was a noise and the plane came into sight. The ambulance and the plane's support vehicle arrived. After the plane landed, Tim got out just shaking his head. The clouds were so low, they couldn't find the airstrip. The pilot ended up going out into the bay, dropping until he could see the water meet the land. He told Tim to count to 10 slowly when the plane began flying over the land because the clouds would block his vision again. When 10 was reached, the pilot did a 90 degree turn, dropping until he could see the runway.

As exciting as the landing was, we had to get into town before it got dark. Tim led the way and Virginia and I followed. We got to the gravel creek. The water looked deeper than it had before. Virginia said she would walk through and see if it was too deep for the bikes. Tim and I began talking, not watching Virginia's struggle with waist-deep water. She got to the other side and yelled, "Come on in, the water's fine!" We did think she meant that the water was not too deep.

Tim decided he would go first. He started his bike and went back about 20 metres so he would have a good run across the creek, which was about 8 or 9 metres across. He revved the bike and took off. I think he would have made it if the creek had been just a metre narrower and perhaps a metre shallower. The bike lost its momentum and the engine died. All we could see was Tim's helmet bobbing as the current carried him towards the sea. He managed to grab hold of a fallen telephone line. We suggested he let go of his bike, but he refused. "I've just paid for it. I'm not letting go! Come and help me get it out."

All Virginia and I could see was Tim's helmet and an arm extended over a wire. Virginia had amazing reflexes and was in the water on her way to save Tim before I had time to decide what to do. Unfortunately, Virginia lost her footing in a pothole and ended up floating past Tim. He grabbed her shirt and she found herself holding onto the telephone wire with him. It was up to me to rescue them.

Laughing hysterically, I launched myself into the water, bent on saving the bike as well as Tim and Virginia. I, too, lost my footing and found myself clinging onto Tim in the middle of the creek. It was getting dark and we had absolutely no idea of what to do. Then we heard a truck. The pilot arrived. His truck's headlights had found my motorbike parked in the middle of the road. He stopped, got out, and we all shouted. Rescue was at hand.

The 4 wheel drive truck drove through the creek and then the pilot waded in. I believe the water had gone down, enough so he wasn't swept off his feet as well. Tim, however, maintains that because he wasn't laughing he was able to concentrate. When he got to us, Tim said, "Save the women first." Much to Tim's dismay, the pilot did. He then went back and pulled Tim and his bike out of the water. We were all loaded into the back of the truck, which didn't have a flap to hold anything in the tray. Tim was just getting in when the pilot reversed to get my bike. This threw Tim back into the water. Eventually, we managed to get both bikes and the three of us back to the school.

The pilot asked where we wanted to be dropped off and we said that we didn't want anyone to see us. "Could you please drop off us off at the staff houses at the school," we pleaded.

Of course, just as the six hundred students were sitting down to supper, the pilot pulled up outside the open air mess. "Is this okay?" he asked. We were the evening's entertainment as we crawled out from the back of the truck and pushed the motorbikes down the road which led to the staff housing.

Tim's bike never ran again.

Sally and Virginia on motorbike

Tim and I spent a lot of time together those final couple of months. Rob, the local entrepreneur, ran the movie house, and we went regularly. Tim sat with a squash racket hitting bats, and I sat beside him watching *Ma and Pa Kettle* or a cowboy Western. We sat in the balcony—it sounds much classier than it was—we were usually the only ones there. Everyone else sat in rows of canvas-backed deck chairs on the floor below.

After spending an evening at the movies, we drove home on our motorbikes. I was sharing a house with a nutritionist so we often ended up chatting quietly outside. On one such evening, Tim produced a ring and asked me to marry him. It turned out Rob had finally broken up with his girlfriend and she had returned the engagement ring. Tim bought the ring and gave it to me.

I accepted but felt that I needed to think things over once I returned to Canada. I had been in Alotau for two years and needed to know if this was the real thing. I also thought it might complicate things for Tim if everyone knew he was engaged. I took the ring and wore it on a chain around my neck. Eventually, I lost it.

I had my ticket home. There was a replacement for me at the school. I returned to Canada to complete my honours degree at Trent.

Tim had come as a teacher and was paid an expatriate's salary plus airfare and bonuses, should he stay for an extended period of time. In the eight months following my departure, Tim was able to save enough money to send me a one way ticket back to Papua New Guinea in June 1977. As I was not returning to a job, I had to sign a paper agreeing to leave the country within eight weeks if there was no marriage. On his part, Tim had to agree to marry me within eight weeks of my arrival in the country or he was responsible for making sure I left the country. Otherwise, he would go to jail.

Once my father found out the conditions, he stepped in and purchased the return air ticket for me. "Don't feel you have to marry him," muttered my father. "Come back if you don't want to." My parents knew that there was every possibility of a wedding but did not know when. I don't think Tim's parents knew anything at all until it was too late.

We were married in a small Anglican Church in Alotau. We wrote and told both sets of parents so they would know the day but would not have enough time to make arrangements to attend. Because Tim's family lived in England and mine in Canada, having a wedding away from both countries made sense to us at the time. There was no my friends, your friends, my family, your family. Everything belonged to both of us.

The Anglican priest published the banns of marriage

for each of the three Sundays preceding the wedding. He insisted that Tim and I be at each of the services when the banns were read, even if he had to wait until we arrived. We were both working at the boarding school and Sunday was the only day we could sleep in. The service began at 9:00 am and was four kilometres away. We were often late and were subject to Father Bodger saying, "Oh, Tim and Sally are here now. We can begin. It's only quarter past nine this time."

Father Bodger had been in PNG on and off since the 1920s. His sister, as it turned out, lived on the same street in Leeds as Tim's parents so he had a sort of kindred affection for Tim and would visit often. When offered tea, he would suggest that perhaps something a little stronger was in order. He was never afraid to voice his disapproval both in and out of church. He would stop a hymn halfway through and say, "No one's singing. Why did you bother coming?"

The wedding was to follow the Anglican church's Book of Common Prayer. As there was nowhere to buy wedding rings in Alotau, we had to order them by mail. We cut bits of string that were the exact size of our fourth finger on our left hands and mailed them to a jeweller's in Port Moresby, the capital city. In a letter we asked for plain gold bands that did not cost more than $50 for each ring. They arrived safely and, more to the point, they fit.

There were more than 600 students at the school and although everyone wanted to attend, the church was not big enough. Only the senior students came to the church service and the other students helped prepare for the wedding reception and joined in the feast. Some of the students participated in the traditional dancing that took place after the meal.

The headmaster provided the processional music through a boom box plugged in at the front of the church. The guests sang a couple of hymns that had been chosen because everyone knew them. The reception was at the school's assembly hall and was a feast of pig, sweet potato, and yam. It was followed by traditional dancing and gift opening. In the eyes of Alotau, we were married.

Tim and Sally at their wedding

Six months later when we visited both sets of parents for the first time we felt they didn't actually believe we were married. We ended up attending special "Blessing of the Wedding" ceremonies at churches in both England and Canada. Then, in the eyes of our parents, we were married.

Christmas 1977 in Sault Ste. Marie Back row: l-r Sally, Tim. Alison, Dad, Mum Front row: l-r Fiona, Hilary

Our honeymoon was unconventional. I'm not sure of the kinds of souvenirs other people bring back from their honeymoons but I'm sure it's not a doughnut shaped rock. But we have one. It sits on the mantelpiece. I do not think anyone has ever asked me what it was. Most people probably just think it's a doughnut that's been sitting around for a long time.

The provincial school examiner (who gave me away when we were married) asked Tim if we would be interested in supervising the national exams at an Anglican girls' high school called Holy Name in Dogura, a mission station about ten minutes flying from where we were living. The exams were being held the week after our wedding and it would mean that we would be able to get away legitimately for a few days before our married life at a boarding school began.

We flew to Dogura on Monday morning, complete with exams, a bottle of sherry for the Headmistress, and two bottles of wine for ourselves. There was not much at

Dogura—the school, a clinic, and a cathedral. I think there was a trade store for everyday bits and pieces. The mission station was not against alcohol but it could not be purchased in the area. Our friend Arty, the examination supervisor, had been over the week before, making certain we had a place to stay as well as a reasonable amount of privacy. Or that was what he told us. Two volunteer teachers who shared a house at the mission moved to another place so we could have the house to ourselves.

By the time we arrived in the late afternoon, the house was immaculate and there were fresh flowers on the dining room table. The Headmistress was very accommodating. "Now, I know you two were just married so don't worry, you can push the two single beds together. Make yourselves comfortable. There's food in the fridge, just help yourselves."

I was totally mortified that this very proper Anglican headmistress had mentioned our sleeping arrangements. It did not seem to bother Tim, who just replied, "Okay then." After thanking us for the bottle of sherry, the Headmistress departed, and we were left alone. I started rummaging around in the kitchen looking for food for supper when a group of four teachers arrived from the school. Together we prepared supper and when it was ready, it appeared that everyone was going to eat with us.

"Perhaps you should get that bottle of wine," I whispered to Tim. He asked if anyone had a corkscrew and was immediately offered two. The first bottle of wine was gone so quickly it was as if it had never been there. After the second was emptied and we declared there was no more, the dishes were done and the coffee was made.

At exactly 9:45pm our guests departed, saying they would be back for breakfast at 6:00am. Any thought we'd had of moving the beds together went out the window at that point. I could not imagine pushing them back before the others arrived. Having reached that conclusion, I made my way outside to use the toilet and did not linger. A recent CUSO newsletter had described another CUSO volunteer sitting in the outhouse minding his own business when the seat gave way.

Tim then proceeded out to the outhouse with a flashlight. For some reason, he thought he should check out the insect life before he used the facility. He shone the flashlight in all the nooks and crannies. He then came back to the house and declared, "I can't possibly use that toilet. There's a spider down the hole that's as big as my hand."

To which I replied, "Why did you shine a light down the hole? Do you really want to know what's down there?"

He then explained his morbid fear of spiders, this from a man who could handle any snake put in front of him. Luckily, there was a tree close by and he used that. "Anything more," he declared, "will have to wait till I get home."

There was a sudden blinking of the inside lights at this point and we were plunged into darkness. It was exactly 10:00pm by our watches and we learned the hard way that the mission generator stopped at 10:00pm and would probably start again at 6:00am. We now under-stood the 9:45pm rush by the teachers. Using the only flashlight we had we managed to get ready for bed and then crawl into our individual beds in separate rooms. There was a wall of woven bamboo between us.

"Goodnight," I said.

"Goodnight," said Tim.

After a few minutes, there was a noise of a door opening.

"Is that you, Tim?" I asked loudly, thinking he was on his way to the toilet again.

"No," whispered his voice through the slats. "I thought it was you."

"Aren't you going to get up and see what it is?" I was beginning to panic as the noise was now that of crumpled paper and dropped dishes.

"If you're worried about it, why don't you get up?" was the reply from my husband of two days.

"I would, but you have the flashlight. Come on, get up," I said encouragingly.

Reluctantly, Tim got up. He pulled a sheet around him and shone the flashlight in front of him. For the first time I heard him mutter the phrase I have since heard so often, "The things I do for you."

Tim crept slowly through his bedroom and into the living room. As he got closer to the kitchen, a snorting noise was heard by both of us. The light from the flash-light bounced off the kitchen walls and onto the side of a pig.

"It's the biggest pig I've ever seen and it's eating the

garbage," exclaimed Tim. "How do you ask a pig to leave?"

In the confusion of the lights going out, neither of us had thought to check the latch on the only door into the house. Pigs in Papua New Guinea are not usually penned so they can search for more food. This one must have smelled the garbage and come to check it out.

Under Tim's direction, the pig decided to leave the house. He dropped the latch, and just to be sure, pushed a chair against the door. We then went back to bed.

In the morning, at 6:00am as promised, the volunteers tried to get into the house for breakfast. They were not able to open the door. As we struggled to get up and dressed before four strangers arrived, we could hear the rude comments about wedding and honeymoons and newlyweds. I kept thinking, if only they knew how far from the truth they were.

Although we had to supervise exams while we were there, we managed to visit the sites and get our souvenir. The church at Dogura had been built in the 1920s.

The priest that married us said that the builders wanted to duplicate St Paul's Cathedral in England but had to settle for something a bit smaller. Inside the church, we saw its walls were decorated with pieces of brick from churches around the world. We found the stairs to one of the towers and climbed to the top. There we found the stones that looked like doughnuts, scattered all over the floor. Tim picked one up, intending to ask someone what they were.

Of course, we returned home, not having asked anyone what the stone was. Eventually, a visiting anthropologist saw it and asked where we had managed to get hold of a killing stone. They were apparently quite rare. He explained that a stick was stuck through the hole in the middle, creating a handle so that animals or people could be killed.

Picked up in all innocence, we now possess a killing stone that had probably been confiscated by the missionaries. Its smooth surface and lustre hide its morbid purpose. It rests on the mantelpiece as a constant reminder of the three-day honeymoon, a pig, and a huge cathedral.

About a month after we were married Tim asked me if I was interested in a boat trip. We had a week off school and Tim wanted to visit some of the students in Suau, an area around the southern tip of Milne Bay. I agreed.

The plan was to get a boat from Alotau, which would take us to Samarai, an island at the mouth of Milne Bay. From there, we would transfer to a smaller boat, which would take us on the three-hour trip to Suau.

From the start, nothing went as planned. We got to the Alotau wharf at 10:00am. The boat was supposed to leave at 10:30 but we ended up waiting until 4:00pm before the boat was ready to leave. We spent the whole time at the wharf because every time we asked someone when the boat was going, the reply was always, 'in a few minutes.'

When we eventually reached Samarai it was almost dark and we realized that we would have to spend the night. Luckily, we had planned for this eventuality and had the keys to an apartment we could use. After we dropped off our knapsacks, we headed to the local club for a drink and some food. The evening was spent in the company of one of the shipping managers in the area who insisted we go back to his house for something to eat. And then, just to round off the evening, he tuned his shortwave radio to the cricket match between Australia and England being played at the famous Lords' cricket ground in England.

I sat in a chair in this man's living room, for hours, watching two grown men press their ears against the radio's speakers trying to get as close as they could to the action. The cricket match went on and on. Despite my continual signals, Tim wanted to stay until the end of the game. Cricket is not a short game and with the time difference I think it ended at about 4:00am. At this point we were invited to spend the night and we slept on a pull-out couch in the man's front room.

We returned to the apartment in the morning, had a shower, changed clothes, and headed down to the wharf, ready to begin our trip. Supplies for a plantation near Suau were still being loaded on the *Misnabeta* and so we found a snack shop and had a breakfast of cold greasy hamburgers and deep-fried sweet potato chips. We returned to the boat to find it still not ready. After lunch, they assured us, it would leave. We wandered around, enjoying the colonial atmosphere of Samarai, and returned to the *Misnabeta* once again. This time we were allowed to board. Then we noticed that all the crew members had enjoyed alcohol as well as food for lunch.

"Tim, let's get off. Everybody's drunk," I whispered.

Tim was worried that we would not get another ride to Suau. "Come on, let's go. These guys know these waters like the back of their hands. Drunk or sober, they'll get us there."

Of course, I allowed myself to be talked into the ride. It was only going to be three hours. What could possibly go wrong?

The *Misnabeta* was a small coastal trading boat. It had a cabin perched on the deck behind the bow that held the traditional maritime wheel and a small bench seat. There was cargo space in the hold. The plantation supplies in the hold included cases of beer, wine, and spirits as well as groceries.

There were about a dozen people in the hold by the time Tim and I boarded. They were all men, primarily plantation workers returning after taking holidays. We were told to sit on the bench behind the wheel and were joined by a primary school inspector. Tim and I were the only non-Papua New Guineans on board. The captain, wearing a yellow hard hat, was in the hold, drinking with his friend. Isaiah, a fellow we knew was originally from Suau, had taken over the wheel, helped by his good friend Captain Morgan.

Once the boat left the relative calm of Samarai harbour and headed to the coast to follow the shoreline, its movement was too much for Tim. Not only was the boat going forwards and backwards, it was also going from side to side. Tim lay on the floor of the cabin with his head protruding out the door, heaving into the sea. I held onto his belt since each time the boat tilted from one side to the other, he was in grave danger of being washed overboard.

After about two hours of tossing and turning, there was a sudden commotion coming from the hold. A man had come halfway out of the hold to throw his beer bottle overboard, but instead, had thrown himself over. The beer bottle miraculously stayed on the deck. When Isaiah heard the shout, he immediately turned the boat and everyone on board began looking for the body. Luckily, we found the man, gasping and spluttering. He was pulled back on board and disappeared below to resume drinking.

We kept going. Another hour passed. It was starting to get dark. Tim was still heaving over the side. I kept looking for the lights of Suau. Darkness fell quickly. The person steering the boat now clutched an empty bottle of rum and said to no one in particular, "I have to turn right at the third light. One, two, where's the third light? I'll start again. One, two ...." Peering out into the darkness, I couldn't see anything. It started to rain and visibility grew less by the minute.

All of a sudden, the boat hit something and stopped moving. The engines were shut off. It was quiet. Tim picked himself off the floor and said to me, "Don't worry We've probably hit a reef. We'll stay here until it's light and help will come." I didn't remind him that no one knew where we were, and I had not seen a radio or a lifeboat.

The engines started up again, and we backed off the reef, making loud scraping noises. Then the engine stopped again, Isaiah yelled something, and the anchor was thrown overboard.

The primary school inspector told us that the captain, wherever he was, had decided we would stay where we were until the rain died down and the lights could be seen. The three of us clambered into the hold, hoping to get food and water, neither of which we'd had since we boarded.

The hold resembled my idea of hell. The entrance to it was covered by a loose piece of torn canvas that blew open and shut in the wind and let in the rain. Everyone in the hold was in various stages of intoxication except for Tim, me, and the primary school inspector. We carefully sat down on a bench nailed to the side of the boat. Bilge water swilled around our feet and boxes of supplies were floating in the water. The hold was lit by a single kerosene lamp, swaying on a nail. We debated getting drunk ourselves but decided it would solve nothing.

All of a sudden the man who had fallen overboard earlier jumped on the person who had pulled him in from the water, screaming, "You took the money out of my pocket! Thief!"

The rescuer said he hadn't. The other man continued to scream at him and then suddenly put his hand in his pocket and brought out a six-inch switchblade and opened it. "Cut me! Go on, I dare you to cut me!" screamed the rescuer. They wrestled for a while on the floor with all of us moving our feet periodically. Then the knife was thrown and stuck in a 44-gallon drum of kerosene which started to leak into the bilge water. The fight ended immediately and the drinking began again.

We found enough fresh water for three cups of coffee heated over a kerosene stove. We decided that the others in the boat were too far gone to appreciate something non-alcoholic and warm. As we drank our coffee, it dawned on us that we were not going to make it. We had been out on the water for almost six hours already. It was only supposed to be a three-hour trip. We had been remarkably stupid even to get on board. We had not told anyone what boat we were going on. Our absence would not be noticed until school began the following week.

For the first time, both of us realized that death was close. We did not do what people in books say they do: write to loved ones, talk about what would be missed. We just accepted our fate, hoping that when the boat sank we would be the first to drown and not be eaten to death by the sharks that were known to be in the surrounding waters. We knew we were going to die and so we went to the front of the boat and lay down on some burlap sacks. They stank of copra, a form of dried coconut. Shortly after, the engine started. Holding hands, we went to sleep, completely resigned to our fate.

The next thing we knew we were jolted awake by the impact of another collision. This time we heard someone shout "Suau" so we thought that we had hit the wharf. When we looked, there was no wharf but a dugout canoe was next to the *Misnabeta*, rocking gently in the water. The man in the dugout motioned us to get in. We clambered over the side of the boat and gently stepped into the canoe and sat down. The smoothest part of the whole trip was that canoe ride to shore. Although we didn't kiss the ground when we felt land beneath our feet, it was wonderful to feel that we had survived. We learned later that the wharf had been destroyed in a storm the previous year. The only thing left were the support posts and that's what we hit.

We were escorted up to the mission house and asked if we wanted a cup of tea. It was 11 o'clock at night. We had had nine hours of hell and a cup of tea sounded like nectar from the gods. The mission house was made of bush material, mainly woven coconut leaves, and was set back on the beach on stilts, about three feet above the ground. A woman arrived carrying an enormous willow-patterned platter loaded with scones and sandwiches. A second woman followed carrying a pot of tea covered with a tea cozy. The women explained that the London Missionary Society's early missionaries had left part of their English lifestyle behind. They were precious items and only brought out for special occasions. The platter and the teapot had even been buried for the duration of World War Two to stop them from being destroyed.

Conversation began. The people in the room spoke English and several of our students arrived. We told the story of our trip: how there was no fresh water, no lifeboat, no radio, and everyone was drunk. Everyone tut-tutted. Discussion then veered towards sleeping arrangements. We were asked if we were married. We said we were. One of the students said that he had been there when we were married. No one believed us until we showed our wedding rings.

Everything was all right after that. There were other visitors in the community for a United Church confer-ence and accommodation was at a premium. We were shown into a room with a double mattress. As we looked around, we noticed other pairs of sleeping bodies. All the married couples slept in the same room so we were allowed to join them.

The next day, the captain of the *Misnabeta* arrived, still wearing his hard hat, to ask for his fare. We had heard that the second bump the night before was from hitting a boat that was anchored on the approach to Suau. Eventually, after much discussion, we paid the man half. We had arrived after all.

A few days later we chartered a small fishing boat to go to a more remote spot and visit other students. As we boarded the boat, we noticed that a small dugout canoe was tied behind the boat. We thought the boat owners were taking it somewhere else. When we arrived at our destination and were waiting for the students, the boat's owner asked if we wanted tea. We accepted and he quickly whipped out a large bottle of water. He said, "That *Misnabeta* was a no good boat. This boat has everything." He went on to explain. "A lifeboat," he said, pointing to the dugout canoe. "Fresh water," and he showed us the bottle. "And," he said, "a radio." And he got out his transistor and turned it on.

In boxes, wrapped in newspaper, in wooden bowls, on top of the fridge, as well as on the mantlepiece in all the houses we have lived in, lie hundreds of shells. They are all Tim's and he is able to describe where and when each shell was purchased or found. They have been packed and repacked many times and have had homes in the Arctic as well as on the Prairies and now on the East Coast. They have been taken to Hutterite schools and remote Northern schools so that children who had never seen the ocean could hear it by holding the shells up to their ears.

I have always blamed Tim's father for the shell collection, as he was the one that demanded a turtle shell when Tim first went to Papua New Guinea. Tony thought it would make a wonderful wall hanging and conversation piece in their English home.

When I first met Tim, he had been in the country for only a few days and had already begun his search. Tim made an announcement one day at early morning assembly: "If anyone knows where I can get a turtle shell, can they please see me after assembly."

There were a few strange looks, but it did work. A few days later one of the students came to Tim at lunch and told him there was a turtle shell at the local market. Tim had just enough time to get to the market and back before afternoon assembly because of his recently acquired Honda 70 motor bike.

When Tim arrived at the market, there was a turtle shell, but the turtle was attached to it. He was afraid that if he didn't buy it, he would never again have another opportunity. The turtle was about the size of a throw cushion and Tim could not carry it and drive the motorbike at the same time. The people at the market didn't want to lose a sale, so they quickly wove some vines together and tied the turtle to Tim's back, its head hanging on his crash helmet.

Afternoon assembly had started by the time Tim

returned. All 600 students and 30 staff turned as they heard the motorbike. As Tim came to a stop, everyone could see the turtle.

Tim had several students assigned to him to work in the art room. Their first job that day was to deal with the turtle, which was unfortunately still alive. After much discussion about the best way to kill the turtle, two students were dispatched to do the dastardly deed and the rest got to work. The turtle killers also removed all the turtle meat and Tim ended the afternoon with his turtle shell and about twenty pounds of white turtle meat.

The next problem was how to clean the shell. There was still 'stuff' attached to it and debate was heated amongst the students as to how best to clean it. Meanwhile, also at Tim's request, the local abattoir had sent over a number of beef bones for Tim's drawing class. These still had 'stuff' attached to them as well. I never discovered who decided to hang the bones and shell in the tree outside Tim's house but I learned the rationale for it. In the tropics, decay happens quickly. Ants are attracted to decay and the theory was that in a couple of days the shell and bones would be picked clean.

One important aspect of the whole process was forgotten. Staff accommodation was close to the school. We all lived in houses, separated by driveways, along a road. The house closest to the school was furthest away from the road, the next house was closest to the road, the third, furthest away again. The designer of the school felt that teachers did not want to look into each other's windows so the houses were staggered. Within 24 hours of the bones in the tree, there was a distinctive smell coming from around Tim's house.

Staff room conversation was very pointed. The agriculture teacher, who was Australian, lived next to Tim and didn't mince words. "You Pommy idiot hanging bones in the trees—you're stinking us out of house and home!" he shouted at Tim after the bones had been up for a day.

On the other side was an English couple dabbling in vegetarianism, who asked politely, "Who died at your house?"

The Papua New Guineans on staff could not understand why anyone would hang a turtle shell in a tree, let alone a number of beef bones They just shook their heads and muttered, "Crazy *dimdim*" (the local word for white people).

By the second day, a petition was circulating amongst staff to have the objects removed from the tree for health reasons. The headmaster called Tim in on the third day and said he would have the day to get rid of the offensive objects. If they were not gone by five o'clock he would arrange for the disposal of the bones. After this announcement, which although held in the headmaster's office could be heard in the staff room, one of the Papua New Guinean staff said that in his village people often buried live seashells they collected. Over time, the insides of the shells decayed and when the shells were dug up several months later, the insides were gone and the person was left with a beautiful and colourful shell. Tim decided that perhaps the same process could be applied to bones and turtle shells.

Tim found two students to help him dig the holes. This time, they took everything a fair distance from the staff houses and the school. The turtle shell and the bones were placed in a hole and covered with dirt and the area was marked with some sticks. Tim was thrilled at the thought of giving the shell to his father.

Six months later Tim returned to the site to uncover the treasures. He could not find the spot. In the tropical rainforest, vegetation can change in a matter of days. He could not tell where the hole had been dug.

After we were married, I found a turtle shell without a turtle in it. I bought it and gave it to Tim's father one Christmas. It was dramatically marked with a hole from where it had been struck with a spear. I'm sorry he never got the other one.

My morbid fear of snakes, I think, goes back to my youth in northern Ontario when I stepped on a garter snake in my bare feet. In Papua New Guinea I never went outside without shoes.

For some reason, all the houses at the first school I went to had wood stoves. I could never understand why they were so popular in the tropics in government housing.

Every afternoon, students at the school would replenish the staff's wood supply and stack it under the house. The house I first lived in had been vacant for a while and the wood had stockpiled. It took me some time before I was ready to use the wood stove regularly.

However, once I discovered that my hot water depended on the wood stove, I lit it every day.

I became an expert at lighting the wood stove in all weathers and used up wood at a rate faster than the students could get it under the house. I began using the stockpile of wood that had been under the house for months. One particular afternoon, I brought a bundle into the house and threw it into the wood space between the stove and the counter. After the fire was going I started throwing the bigger pieces in. Unfortunately, a snake called a 'sleeping sam' had taken up residence in this particular pile of wood and was not happy when I went to throw him with some other pieces of wood on the fire.

Naturally, when the wood started to move, I panicked, screamed, and hurled the wood, snake and all, out of the house.

That was my first encounter. I learned to pick the wood up piece by piece and asked other people to pick up pieces that had been stacked for long periods of time. Each time I picked up a piece of wood I would bang the next piece, hoping that the snake would hear me coming and disappear. I had been in the country, singing and clapping my way in the bush so that the snakes would go away, for over five years before I learned that snakes don't have ears and only sense your presence through vibration. I then changed my tactics and started stomping.

Tim arrived about 1 ½ years after me to teach expressive arts. His classroom was a cement slab protected from the sun and the rain by a corrugated iron roof. He introduced the art of silk screen printing and within a month had a group of students who met daily to print t-shirts for businesses and sporting organizations around town.

One afternoon, as he was working with a group of students the rain began to fall heavily on the roof. The tropical downpour stopped conversation but everyone kept working. Tim was setting up a screen and happened to look up. All the students were standing in the rain trying to get his attention, shouting as loudly as they could.

Tim cupped his hand to his ear and yelled, "What's wrong?"

In response the students pointed to a snake that was making a bee-line towards Tim. The only part of its body touching the ground was its tail and it was moving quickly.

Tim told me later, "I had two choices. If I had run out and joined the students in the rain I felt I would lose face. The students would not respect me and I would look foolish." I, of course, had been in the country eighteen months longer and knew that respect would not have been lost if he'd run out. It would have been perfectly normal. What was abnormal was what he did.

After picking up a stick and a saucepan he went towards the snake and managed to direct the snake into the saucepan and put the lid on. At this point the students came back into the classroom again, muttering "Crazy dimdim."

Meanwhile, Tim took the saucepan into the school office, anxious to find out what kind of snake he had captured. A local teacher was waiting for a phone call and sitting in the secretary's chair, protected from Tim by a shelf that was chest high. Tim put the saucepan on top of the shelf and asked the teacher to look in it and tell him what it was. He took a glance and leapt over the shelf. I guess adrenalin makes you do incredible physical feats—he was only 5 foot 6 inches. His parting words were shouted as he disappeared from sight, "Get rid of it!"

There was no one else to ask and like a small boy whose great plans had gone up in smoke, Tim slunk out of the office. He walked down a path that led to the bush and let the snake go. It quickly slithered away.

Years later, we met up with a snake expert who was visiting. The expert was pontificating, explaining when snakes were most dangerous. "You have to be really careful if a snake's body is upright and he's moving very quickly, only his tail touching the ground. It is probably a poisonous snake."

Shortly after we were married, I discovered that Tim's delight in snakes had not waned. Some Papua New Guinean friends had left our house when all of a sudden the wife came running back inside.

"Quick, give me your bush knife. There's a snake on the road!" She shouted. Everyone always had a bush knife or machete next to their wooden stove.

As I went to get it, Tim started asking questions. "What kind of snake is it?"

Junie replied much as I would, "I don't know and I don't care."

"Well, what colour is it?" Tim persisted.

"Tim, it's almost dark outside. I can't tell," said an exasperated Junie. "I've got to take the knife to Rob."

Tim couldn't resist. He followed Junie outside and

saw the snake continuing to cross the road. He managed to talk Junie and Rob out of killing it and came running back inside. "Quick, come out and hold the flashlight while I catch it. Norman will love it. It's a D'Albertis python, Norman doesn't have one." Tim was practically dragging me out the door in his excitement.

Norman was a Canadian, recently arrived on staff, who collected snakes. He and his partner had a number of snakes that lived in their house. It was rumoured that the snakes would actually crawl into their bed during the night, looking for warmth.

"There's no way on God's earth I'm coming out to hold the flashlight!" I shouted back. "Find another sucker."

Luckily, the deputy headmaster was home and he came bounding out of his house, ready to aid and abet. "We caught lots of snakes at my last school," he said excitedly in his broad Australian twang. "I taught in the science labs and we always had snakes in terrariums. The kids would tip 'em out, clean the cages. Then they'd pick up the snakes by the tails with one hand the snakes would go rigid. They'd run their other hand along the snake's body and grip it behind the head. Then the snake would be put back in the terrarium."

Tim listened to this and replied, "You've got to be kidding." He felt that a three-metre python was not quite the same as a snake in a classroom that fit in a terrarium.

The Australian dismissed Tim's scepticism. "You know the story of Aaron's rod in the Bible—where the snake turns into a rod because Moses touches it? Well, that's how it works."

With some trepidation Tim headed off into the bush, leading the way to where the snake was resting, clutching the flashlight in one hand and a burlap sack to put it in in the other. According to Tim's description, the snake was a perfect D'Albertis python; its colour was so black it was almost blue. If you had a passion for snakes, this was a beautiful sample.

Tim was going to catch the snake, using a more traditional approach. "Hold the flashlight," he ordered Alan, the Australian, "and I'll grab it behind its head, run my hand over its body, hold it by the tail, and then dump it in the sack."

The only problem was that Alan wanted to display that his method worked. "Ooh, come on, Tim. Let me do it my way. It's much easier than yours. Don't you believe me?" asked Alan.

So reluctantly, Tim took the flashlight and Alan grabbed the snake by the tail. Tim said later that if he hadn't seen it with his own eyes, he wouldn't have believed it. The three metre python turned into a heavy three metre stick. Alan started to run his hand along the snake's body and slowly he realized he had a problem.

He got about halfway along the snake and ran out of arm. He still had about four feet of snake to go before he reached the head.

"The snakes in the science room must have been shorter. What the hell should I do?" He asked my husband. Tim was of no help as he was bent over double he was laughing so hard.

Eventually, Alan loosened his grip on the middle of the snake, hoping to be able to slide his hand quickly along the body of the snake so he could grip behind the head. The moment he loosened his grip the snake relaxed and its head dropped and went between Alan's legs. It was pretty angry and as it began trying to strike Alan in a sensitive area, he threw the snake high in the air. Both men beat a hasty retreat.

Norman never got his d'Albertis python but still ended up with a great collection of snakes living in his house with him. I only heard this; I never visited.

5. Passam National High School, Wewak 1979 – 1980

Me outside our house at Passam 1979 - 1980

At the end of 1978, we left Alotau and moved to the northwest of Papua New Guinea, close to the border with Irian Jaya. Passam National High School had been open for a year and taught Grade 11 and 12 students from across the country who were the top 2% academically. Tim had been appointed to teach Expressive Arts and I was to teach English and history/politics.

Passam was about 20 km to Wewak on the coast and any shopping we needed meant a trip down the road. The motorbikes weren't very practical and Tim and I purchased our first vehicle. It was a brown Toyota 1000 truck with two bucket seats in the front and a small cargo area in the back. Tim had never learned to drive in England because he'd never needed to, but the purchase of our truck spurred his resolve and within days, he had his "P" plates. In Papua New Guinea, a new driver must show these on the vehicle he is driving for a year after getting his driver's licence.

When Tim's mother, Betty, and brother Michael who was 14 at that time, arrived for a visit, we made all kinds of plans to get them out and about, using our new truck. We decided to take them to the Sepik River, which was about two hours away from the school, hire a canoe with a motor, visit a couple of villages and then return. We also took two of our old students from Alotau with us who were visiting us for their holidays.

On the way back from the village, the motor went dead in the middle of the river and Albert, the man steering the canoe, needed to get it to shore to fix it. I figured that someone had to get to the front of the canoe so that when it reached the bank it could be pulled up. Tim's family had not spent the time I had in canoes, growing up as I did in northern Ontario, and I was quite happy to walk along the gunnels of the canoe with everyone ducking their head so I could be the one to jump on shore.

That was when I found out that swimming in the crocodile-infested waters of the Sepik River was not an occupation of choice for the Goddard family, and Betty thought that was what would happen if I proceeded. As I walked along the gunnels all I could hear was Betty shouting, "What the hell do you think you're doing? Sit down for God's sake!" Which of course I did because she was a definite voice of authority after years of being a matron in a Leeds hospital.

The boat bumped onto the bank without me jumping off the bow. Albert jumped into the water and walked to the shore and then pulled the canoe up himself. He soon fixed the engine and we were on our way.

When the time came to return home, Tim's mother decided to sit in the back of the truck with Michael, rather than sitting in the front with either her son or myself. She was still angry about the danger she felt I had placed her and her family. We were only about ten minutes from home when we heard the lublublub of a flat tire. Although the truck was new, we soon discovered that coral roads destroyed tires quickly.

None of us had ever changed a flat tire. Tim didn't want his mother to know that he had no idea what to do. My job was to feed him the information from the driver's manual in a way that Betty wouldn't suspect that Tim knew nothing. Tim's mother climbed out of the back of the truck and with her hands on her hips said, "Tony (Tim's father) has been driving for nearly thirty years and has never had a flat tire." The focus of her anger had finally left me.

I asked Tim if he had found the spare tire under the tray of the truck. He got on his back and got under the truck. I then suggested that he unscrew the butterfly clip that was holding the tire up with a metal A-frame.

After the bolt was undone he held onto the frame and came out from under the truck. He turned, and kneeling towards the tire, dropped the frame. The snake that had taken up residence in the tire was obviously disturbed and tried to get away. Tim's mother took off like an Olympic runner bent on breaking a world record. One of the students threw the tire iron at the snake, decapitating it. Tim was just starting to stand up when the headless snake brushed against the side of his face. It was pretty funny. We managed to change the tire and pick up Tim's mother who was about a kilometre away.

For years afterwards, whenever Betty came to stay we would tell the story. At one point Betty had had enough. We were sitting around the dinner table, telling her snake story and she said, "Enough. I brought my diary from that year and I want to read my side." She read out her version of the story, which was remarkably similar to ours until we got to the part when the snake came out from the tire. All her diary said was, 'Chaos ensued.' She wasn't wrong but she did leave out her run.

My father turned 60 in November 1979, and we decided that we would telephone him on his birthday and tell him his first grandchild was on the way, due sometime in May. The only way we could do this was to use the two-way radio in the school office but first we had to figure out what time and day it was in Canada. Eventually, after much discussion and arithmetic, we thought that if we called in the late afternoon on the 14th of November, it would be breakfast time, the morning of my father's birthday, in Sault Ste Marie, Ontario. We called the operator and gave him the phone number. But we couldn't just say we'd like to call Canada. We had to use the phonetic alphabet so the operator could understand the number. Today, very few people use a telephone operator, but in 1979, if you wanted to call outside of the country, you had to dial 0 for the operator. The school had a two-way telephone so you had to say "over" every time you finished a sentence.

I said, "I'd like to call Canada, please. Over."

The operator said, "How do you spell that? Over."

I said, "C for Charlie, A for alpha, N for November, A for Alpha, D for Delta, A for alpha. Over." The operator said, "Ah, Canada. What number please? Over."

I then gave the operator the number, and eventually, we were connected. My father answered the phone. He said, "Hello."

However, he didn't know about saying 'over'. I said, "Dad, it's me, Sally. Over."

He said immediately, "Is there anything wrong?"

I said, "You have to say 'over' when you have finished talking and are waiting for a reply. Over." My father said, "I haven't done that since the war. Over."

So I wished him a happy birthday and told him the good news.

He asked, "When's the baby due? Over."

I responded, "Sometime towards the end of May, the beginning of June. Over."

He then asked where I was going to have the baby. I hadn't really thought about that.

I said, "I guess I will have it here. People have babies here all the time. It should be fine. Over."

We didn't talk for long. My father was pleased with the news but concerned about health care facilities. Later, he wrote and said, "Ninety percent of the time it doesn't matter where you have the baby. It will be born. But 10 percent of the time you need to be close to a hospital." I was young and healthy. I was sure nothing would go wrong.

We went on leave in December and went first to my parents' home in Sault Ste. Marie, Ontario, Canada, for Christmas.

Christmas 1979 Back row, l-r: Fiona, Alison, Tim, Sally Front row, l-r: Elizabeth, Hilary (Fred the dog), Mum, Dad

We hadn't brought much with us, but my family made sure the first grandchild was not going to be deprived, no matter where we lived. As a result my mother 'lent' us a suitcase and it was loaded down with baby stuff.

While in the Soo, I had visited the obstetrician who mentioned the fact that I shouldn't lift heavy objects. It wasn't that I lifted a lot of heavy things but Tim would miss my help. When we left to fly to England, Tim struggled with two large, heavy suitcases as well as some plastic shopping bags that had last minute things shoved in them that we couldn't possibly manage without. I carried my purse.

When we arrived in Heathrow, we decided to take the new Tube line from Heathrow to King's Cross. Then we would catch the train to Leeds where Tim's parents lived. All the luggage was loaded onto a cart and we proceeded to navigate our way. Tim bought two tickets for the Heathrow-King's Cross section and two more for the King's Cross-Leeds return. Obviously the two return tickets from King's Cross to Leeds were the more valuable. Tim put all four tickets in the breast pocket of his shirt.

Then we proceeded through the turnstile towards the train that would take us to King's Cross. The luggage cart had to be left and all your luggage was supposed to fit through a rectangular metal bar while you walked through the turnstile and claimed your luggage on the other side. I walked through, carrying my purse, then turned to watch Tim. The plastic shopping bags were no problem. The overnight bags fit and eventually returned to their original shape. But the suitcases wouldn't go under the bar. Tim lifted the handle of the first one, and using a pivot step attempted to lift the suitcase over the bar. Unfortunately, the suitcase stayed on one side and the handle went on the other. Then, he grasped the suitcase on both sides and threw it over. Rather than using the handle of the other suitcase, he did the same thing to it. Then he walked through and squeezed the handle back on the first one. We looked up and saw a sign, 'Passengers with heavy luggage are advised to take an alternate route to the city'.

Tim struggled down to the Tube and eventually we boarded and stacked all the luggage against the far door. We figured that as the other door was open at Heathrow, that would be the door that opened all the way to King's Cross. Unfortunately, we were wrong. I think there were 23 stops and each time the door we had the luggage against opened and Tim had to scramble to move it. It was also rush hour and people were trying to get to work. We didn't meet many sympathetic business people.

In those days at King's Cross, there was an incredibly steep long wooden-slatted escalator that took people from the Tube station to the train station. I went ahead and Tim followed, a suitcase in each hand, plastic shopping bags under each arm. We were about halfway up when I heard Tim say, "Oh, shit!" as the suitcase that had already lost its handle once, slipped from Tim's grasp. Once again, Tim was left holding the handle as the suitcase started falling back down the escalator. Surprisingly, no one touched it or picked it up so that it could go back up. The whole of London stepped to one side and watched the suitcase fall to the bottom of the escalator. Someone picked it up then and put it to one side.

Meanwhile, Tim got to the top, dropped the other suitcase and all the plastic shopping bags and raced back down the escalator to reclaim our suitcase. He arrived back where I was and I said that because of all the excitement I had to go to the bathroom. However, in order to get to the bathroom, which was in the train station, I had to present my Heathrow-King's Cross ticket at the barrier that separated the Tube station from the train station. Tim dug in his pocket and gave me one, then said, "For Godsake, find a porter to help with the luggage. I can't do this any more."

I arranged to meet him just past the barrier. There were then three steps up to the train station. When I returned with a porter, Tim was on his hands and knees, looking through a huge pile of tickets.

"What are you doing?" I could barely ask.

"You're not going to believe this," he said. "I thought if I put my ticket between my teeth and picked up all the luggage, I would be able to walk through the barrier and the ticket collector would be able to take the ticket without me putting everything down.

He then looked at a ticket and said, "I don't believe it. I found it."

Instead of putting the Heathrow-King's Cross ticket in his mouth, he mistakenly put one of the expensive King's Cross-Leeds return tickets. They were the same colour and size, and the ticket collector took it. After Tim had walked through the barrier and was waiting for me, he checked the two tickets in his pocket and realized his mistake. He explained his problem to the ticket collector, who looked at him and proceeded to dump the morning's tickets on the floor. "If you can find it, it's yours," he said.

While all this was happening, the porter and his trolley were patiently waiting at the top of the three steps leading from the train station to the Tube station. Tim asked him to come and help.

"I can't come down the steps, sir," said the porter. "It's not allowed."

Tim had reached a point where nothing phased him. He carefully picked up the suitcase with the temperamental handle and presented it to the porter. He went back down and got the other suitcase, carried it up, and returned to get the plastic bags. Then we followed the porter to the train.

The porter couldn't do enough for us. He told us he would get the luggage on the train and he would find us the best seats. I think he had heard my accent and was hoping for a substantial North American tip.

We finally got to the right train, right car. I got on and found us a seat while Tim supervised the luggage. The porter carefully put the plastic shopping bags on the roof rack. He then took one of the suitcases, marked heavy by the airline, and threw it onto the train. He then took the other suitcase and with a heaving motion attempted to duplicate what he had done with the first suitcase. He was left holding the handle. The suitcase remained on the platform.

Tim, of course, didn't waste a moment. "How did you do that? You've broken my suitcase! We have to travel a long way. How am I going to carry it? And I suppose you want a tip?"

The poor porter lifted the suitcase on the train and kept saying, "I'm terribly sorry, sir, terribly sorry," as he handed the handle back to Tim. Once again the handle was squeezed into place and we resumed our journey. The suitcase became known as the world's largest clutch bag.

Our return flight to Papua New Guinea took us through Hong Kong. We booked a room at the Peninsula Hotel for two nights. A green Rolls-Royce picked us up at the airport and loaded our suitcases and plastic bags. It was otherworldly. We went to the floating gardens in the harbour for dinner and found ourselves in a restaurant where we were the only dimdims. They seated us at a corner table so our eating habits would not disturb the others. It was a wonderful evening and on our return the suitcases had been unpacked and a teddy bear my parents had given us for the baby rested between the pillows on the bed. When we returned to the airport in the same car, the driver told us to wait in the car and he stood in line and checked us in and brought us our boarding passes. Airport travel hasn't been the same since.

During my first and second trimester, I visited the prenatal clinic in Wewak monthly. It was about 20 km on a dirt road that often could only be accessed by a 4-wheel drive vehicle. We traded in the Toyota truck for a Suzuki 4 wheel drive vehicle that sounded like a lawn mower. By my third trimester, the clinic was worried that I wasn't putting on enough weight. I was instructed only to teach, not to participate in any other activities. Teachers were expected to work three afternoons a week supervising work parade.

In those days, a woman would get 6 weeks off when she was pregnant. You could take time off before the birth and then subtract it from the time off after. I decided to work until the end of the term, and then take the following six weeks off.

Sally in Wewak, April 1980

On Monday, April 29th. I drove down to Wewak for my weekly prenatal checkup. The doctor was concerned that the baby was in the wrong position. There was no ultrasound so he did an x-ray. It confirmed that the baby was not going to come out easily. The doctor was worried about complications and felt that I needed to see a specialist. The closest one was in Madang, about an hour's flying time away. Tim and I wanted to delay the trip. We didn't think the baby was due until the end of May. My mother was arriving on May 24th. However, the medical people convinced us that time was of the essence. The health department provided us with plane tickets but we were on our own for accommodation and food. We arrived at the Wewak airport on Tuesday, April 30th. The plane was in but there were no seats available, even though we had tickets. There was a Japanese tour group waiting to board the plane. Wewak had been the site of the largest Japanese airbase in New Guinea during World

War II so it was on the tourist route for many Japanese people. The airline agent was an ex-student of ours and he stopped one Japanese couple from getting on the plane so Tim and I could have seats. The couple was promised seats on the next flight and a free lunch. What we didn't know was that the airline was expecting a strike later on that day. The plane we left on was the last one to arrive in Wewak for five days. I have always wondered about what might have happened if we had missed that flight.

We arrived in Madang, rented a car, and found a hotel room. The hotel was right on the water and a little extravagant but it would only be for a day or two. Our appointment with the specialist was not until the next day and we decided to be tourists. We went to the Coastwatchers' Tower, a memorial built to those Australians and Papua New Guineans who lost their lives sending radio messages about Japanese movements during World War II. We ended our afternoon at the Madang Teachers' College where several of our graduating students had gone. It was wonderful to see them settled and happy with their career choices.

When we returned to the hotel, we discovered that the airline that had bought us to Madang was now on strike. We weren't too worried as we figured we could always use one of the smaller airlines to get us back to Wewak. It would take longer and would have more stops, but it could be done. The next morning I saw the specialist. He checked things out and said he felt it would be another month before the baby arrived. Tim said, "So we'll come back in a month?" The specialist replied, "No, you can come back in a month. Your wife must stay here." There was a long pause before he continued, "If you can't find a place to stay, she can always stay at the hospital until the baby comes." The doctor told me to come back in a week.

Tim and I left his office, shocked by the developments. What were we going to do? The hotel we were in was lovely for a couple of nights, but it was too expensive for a long-term arrangement. We started looking. The Madang Country Women's Association advertised its guesthouse for 'women in distress'. That described our plight. Of course, when we got there, there were no vacant rooms. We wandered around Madang that afternoon, finding the hotels too expensive, and the guest houses and hostels full. We eventually gave up looking and wandered over to a corner store to buy a newspaper, in which, we thought, might be a solution.

Out of the blue came a voice, "What are you two doing here?" It was our old bank manager. Tim gave him a quick rundown of our situation. When he had finished, this kind man suggested that we go to his house and meet his wife. This bank manager had a lovely home, overlooking the sea. There was an extra bedroom and bathroom they weren't using. His wife was delighted she would have company. Tim had already discovered that a boat left the Madang Harbour on Friday morning, as he had to go back to work, so we arranged that I would be picked up from the hotel when Tim had gone. Things were looking up. Tim would return to Madang when I went into labour, probably at the end of May. We went back to the hotel and talked about the next few weeks. I said, "It would be so much easier if the baby was born tonight." And, lo and behold, that's what happened.

I felt that labour had started later in the evening. At 10:00pm, the specialist suggested we come to the hospital. By 10:30, I was ushered to a room by a nurse whose sister was a student at our school. The specialist arrived, checked things and declared I was in labour and the safest avenue was a caesarian.

The doctor moved quickly. "Send the ambulance out to find the operating staff," he said to the nurse. She left and he told us that it would take a while before everyone was in place. "We don't often operate at night so we don't keep the staff here. They know they are on call but we have to find them. No one has a telephone. Usually, if people aren't at home, they might be at the movies or visiting friends. Don't worry. The ambulance will find them."

Just after midnight on May 2nd 1980, they wheeled me outside to an adjacent building that housed the operating room. The last thing I remember is looking at the blackboard on the wall where they had written the total number of sponges they had. Next to that column was another, titled 'used'. It was blank.

Tim told me later that the baby was out within 5 minutes. She weighed 2.3 kg and, of course, was perfect. It took longer for me to leave the operating room so Tim had time to look at the nursery and then return to find me. Once he knew both of us were okay, he returned to the hotel and explained to the night clerk what had happened and asked if he could make a phone call to my parents in Canada and his parents in England. As it turned out, the night clerk had also been a student of ours and he couldn't do enough. Tim was terrified of the phone bill, but the hotel clerk only charged him for 2 local calls.

My mother in Sault Ste Marie, Ontario, was thrilled because she thought she had a May Day grandchild. What she hadn't taken into account was the fact that although it was the afternoon of May 1st in Canada when Tim called, it was actually early in the morning of May 2nd in Papua New Guinea because of the International Date Line.

We had nothing with us for the baby to wear. We hadn't thought of a name. We didn't have a crib or a car seat or toys. It wasn't long before people started to arrive at the hospital with things for the baby. Papua New Guineans use the word 'wantok' to describe a person who is from your family, your village, or your language group. It didn't matter that Tim and I were not Papua New Guinean. Relations of students we had taught, students from the teachers' college, and the bank manager and his wife all brought clothing to the hospital.

Naming her was more difficult. We had to have a name before we left the hospital. Tim and I each made lists separately and them compared them. There was not a lot of common ground. As teachers we were also aware of the problems created for children with non-traditional names. I was reading about Nicholas and Alexandra–the story of the last Tsar and Tsarina of Russia. We feminized Nicholas to Nichola, Kathleen was my mother's name, and Sarah was the name of one of my oldest friends. By the weekend, the planes were flying again and we were able to fly back to Wewak. We borrowed a crib and Nichola settled in as though she had been there forever.

My mother had booked her ticket to arrive in time for the birth but in actual fact, the baby had already arrived. She made it for the christening,

l-r: Sally holding Nichola, Kathleen

One particular afternoon, we were later than normal getting home from school. Tim suggested it would be better if he drove the babysitter home while I made supper and got the baby ready for bed. I, of course, saw red, and felt that he had just suggested it so that he could have a relaxing drive while I hustled around, doing all the things that needed to be done. I won the argument and took the keys and left for the village with the babysitter.

We had just passed the gates of the school and were out on the main road when I heard the lublublub noise associated with a flat tire. I pulled over to the side of the road, cursing. The roads were coral and flat tires were a common occurrence. The jack was stored under the front seat, or was supposed to be stored under there. I couldn't find it.

Having made the point before I left the house that I was perfectly capable of taking the babysitter home, I didn't feel that I could go back and ask Tim where the jack was. I could handle this. The mission station was on the other side of the road and I felt sure that the priest would lend me a jack. I walked up the hill to talk to the priest. He was very obliging but only had the jack that came with his coffee truck. He thought it might be a bit big. I shrugged off his concerns and walked back to the car with the jack over my shoulder.

I must confess to never having changed a tire myself before. I have stood by and watched many being changed but I had never done any of the nuts and bolts stuff. I knew there were two holes, one on each side of the car, where the end of the jack should be placed. As the flat tire was on the passenger side of the car, I placed the jack on that side. I pulled the handle of the jack once and nothing happened. I pulled again. Because I'd moved the car over to the side of the road, the driver's side was lower than the passenger's. When I pulled the second time, the whole car tipped over on its side, almost in slow motion. I could see it happening but was powerless to stop it.

Disaster always attracts a crowd and within minutes village people and school children had arrived to gape at what I had done. Not wasting any time, one man climbed on the side of the car and took off the flat tire. Another man got the spare and passed it up to him. It was attached and before I knew it, a group of men righted the car. I thanked them, returned the jack, got in the car, and drove away.

Although I told Tim about the flat tire, it was months before I told him how the tire was changed.

Our school was in an earthquake zone. The newer buildings were constructed using special techniques that made them more earthquake tolerant. No one on staff really gave a lot of thought to earthquake safety. Every now and again, there would be a soft shaking and it was often mistaken for someone shaking their leg or coming up the stairs.

The staff houses were all built in a line which followed the road up a hill. The view from the balconies was lovely. Each house looked over the school gardens and if you looked to the left, the school itself. Each house was separated by a driveway and a small embankment. School started at 7:30 in the morning and continued until 1:30 in the afternoon, then lunch and then two hours of school service in the afternoon. For the two years I was at this school, I was teacher-in-charge of the poultry. Because it was a brand new project, the students and I first had to build the pens, then get the chicks. Ultimately, we supplied the mess with fresh meat and the staff and students with fresh eggs, but it took a while to establish. After supper, the students would have study time, then, literally, lights out.

After Nichola was born and I went back to work, we both had to get up early, usually before the generator came on at 6 am. As the sun rose, I would feed the baby and watch the day begin. One morning, the alarm went off and I tried to get out of bed. The house was moving so much, it was difficult. I woke Tim up and mentioned earthquake. He immediately said, "Grab the baby and go outside. If you don't get out in the first thirty seconds it doesn't matter any more."

In those days, we didn't wear pyjamas and I said, "But I don't have any clothes on." To which he replied, "It doesn't matter. It's an emergency. No one will notice." I struggled into the baby's room and carried her to the living room when I happened to glance back. There was Tim, wrapped in our orange bedspread and trying to lift a four-drawer filing cabinet over his shoulder.

"What are you doing," I stupidly asked, jealous of the bedspread.

"The passports are in here. I saving them," he replied.

"They're on the desk. I took them out yesterday," I said, and watched as he dropped the cabinet.

The house had stopped shaking. We looked at each other. "How come you got the bedspread?" I asked.

Meanwhile there was chaos in other staff houses as well. The couple who lived beside us had no children and both raced out and got well away from their building. Phil told us later that both he and his wife tried to dress themselves, terrified that at any moment the power would come on. So would our outside light, illuminating Phil and Jane.

In the house next to Phil and Jane's there was a new English recruit, his wife, and their three year old daughter. They didn't know what to do, so they all got under the bed. Other friends of ours raced outside and then had a loud argument over who was going to go back in and get their four year old.

The earth stopped shaking but the water in the tanks outside everyone's houses kept sloshing and the Coleman lamp kept swinging backwards and forwards for quite a while!

6. KIRIWINA HIGH SCHOOL, THE TROBRIAND ISLANDS 1981 - 1982

Tim and I were asked to return to Milne Bay to begin a high school at Losuia on the Trobriand Islands. We discussed it for about a nano second. As Tim pointed out to me, "How often do you get to build a school from the ground up?"

Tim was appointed principal, I was to teach Grade 7 English, Social Studies and Home Economics. Another teacher was appointed to handle Math and Science. I don't think either of us realized the challenges that lay before us. Our job was to build a high school so that children finishing elementary school would not have to leave home to go to the mainland for high school. Places in the high schools on the mainland were allocated by a quota system based on examination marks and location. There were never enough places for all the qualified students, so many students from the Trobs never made it to high school.

Nichola was 8 months old when we landed on the gravel airstrip at Losuia which had an aid post, a police station, a post office with a radio telephone, and a trade store. We were the only non-native people living in Losuia, although there was a Catholic mission and a small hotel further out of town, both run by Australians. There was no running water or electricity for the two years we were there.

Our first house was at the crossroads of the community and we were the new people in town. We didn't have any curtains and our house became a reality television show for the community. People would sit on the grass outside our house and watch our meal preparations as well as our child management skills.

We had only been in the house for a short a few days when the unexpected happened. I fed Nichola, washed her, and put her to bed. It was just after 6 pm and it was almost dark. She refused to lie down and sleep. I shut the door to her room and came out to the living room, leaving her crying.

Tim said, "I think we should pick her up."

I replied, "No, then she'll think we will pick her up every time she cries. We don't want to spoil her. Let's just leave her."

We went out and sat on the porch of the house, watching the sunset. All of a sudden we heard the back door open. We went back inside and a woman rushed past us carrying Nichola. She said, "We don't let our babies cry here." As they disappeared down the back steps, Tim and I looked at each other. We were too stunned to move. "Where do you think she's taken her?' I asked Tim.

Tim said, "She can't have gone far. It is an island. I'll go next door and see what Alan suggests." Alan was the primary school inspector, his wife was one of the nurses at the aid station. Tim found the woman and Nichola at Alan's house. Nichola was happily playing in the dirt with the other children. The woman proceeded to lecture Tim on the evils of letting children cry. She let him take Nichola back but warned him that she would do it again if she heard Nichola crying. We got coverings for the windows and were very careful to make sure Nichola didn't cry in the evenings.

Eventually, we moved house and found ourselves further back from the road, but we continued to make sure she didn't cry herself to sleep. When Nichola eventually moved to a bed, one of us would always lie down beside her until she went to sleep, always wary that the crazy lady would hear her crying and come and get her again.

Over time, we settled into life at Losuia. During the week, Tim and I would go to working, dropping Nichola off at Rose and Ernest Goweli's house in the village. She was treated like their own daughter, fed the food of the village, taken to all the celebrations, and watched like a hawk. She was the only blond child on the island. Everyone wanted to touch her skin and feel her hair because it was so different than everyone else's.

House at Losuia

As Nichola learned to walk and talk, she also learned to speak Kiriwinian. Everyone except Tim and I and an Australian nun, Sister Helen, spoke to her in Kiriwinian. She had very few toys because there was nowhere to buy them. She played with pots and pans, sticks and stones, and enjoyed the beaches on the weekends.

We had no running water and no electricity. There was a bathtub, a shower, a toilet and a sink in the house. In years gone by, there must have been enough fuel to run the generator, which provided electricity for Losuia. If the electricity ran long enough, water could be pumped through the pipes and into the house. That never happened while we lived there. In the early evening, I would put a saucepan full of water on the gas stove to heat. I would then pour it and some cold water in a red bowl on the porch. Nichola would have a bath and then I would get the bath water and fill the bucket shower so I could have my own wash. I would catch the water in another bucket for Tim. He would put the water back in the shower bucket and have a shower while I put Nichola to bed. Tim would catch his water in a bucket and before we went to bed, he would flush the toilet with it.

The only fresh water we had came from the rain tank beside our house. The tank was 1000 gallons and had to last us from one rainfall to the next. It was never full and having enough fresh water was always a worry. My sister Alison visited us while we were on Kiriwina. One day we came back from school to find her sitting by the tank, shaving her legs. The tap was fully opened and water was pouring out. Tim was so furious he could hardly speak. I turned off the tap and reminded Alison that we were very low on water. She was leaving the next day and responded, "I might meet someone on the way home."

May 2, 1981 Nichola's 1ˢᵗ birthday celebrated with balloons and whistles sent from Canada. Photo courtesy JT Goddard

Because we had no electricity, the fridge that was in the house when we moved in was really a cupboard where we stored food. If we gave Nichola a bottle in her crib, it was an invitation to all the cockroaches and ants to come and join her. Rose, the woman who looked after Nichola, suggested that we put the legs of the crib in tin cans of water. The tin cans had to be big enough so that the insects couldn't reach the crib legs. We just had to remember to change the water often so mosquitoes wouldn't use it as a breeding area.

Eventually, the Education Department issued us with a kerosene fridge, which meant our food choices expanded. We had a lot of canned food shipped by boat from the mainland. We had tinned hot dogs, chicken, and ham as well as tinned vegetables. When we opened the tin of chicken, a whole chicken slid out, covered in a gelatin-like substance. It would sit on a plate and as the gelatin fell off, the wings and the legs would sort of spring into place. We had 2 gas burners on the top of the stove that worked. The oven never did. A previous tenant had tried to burn wood in the oven and had wrecked it.

We would buy fresh food from people who came to the house: sweet potatoes, yams, and tapioca. The students built gardens and we could buy greens and tomatoes from them. There was always fish, coconuts, papayas, bananas, and green oranges. Nichola never had fresh milk, it was all powdered, and she ate what we ate because there was no baby food. I mashed everything with a fork until she could chew.

One night, just after midnight, Nichola woke, crying. Tim got out of bed and went next door to Nichola's room and lay down on the bed with her. Both of them fell asleep. I awoke just after one, smelling beer in the bedroom. All I could think of was how strange it was for Tim to have a beer at this time of night. When I opened my eyes, I could see a strange man in the room. I didn't actually scream but I called, "Tim, there's somebody in our room!"

Normally, Tim would never have woken with me just calling out to him. Something made him jump out of the bed in Nichola's room and back into ours. Just as he came through the door- way, the man who had been standing there, looking at me, raised his arm and struck Tim with a small axe. Luckily, it was our axe and not very sharp. It glanced off Tim's head and landed in his shoulder.

Tim shouted at me, "Get the flashlight."

We always kept one by the side of the bed. It seemed to take me forever to find it. Meanwhile, the guy had dropped the axe and Tim had wrestled the man to the floor. Holding him by his ears and his hair, Tim banged his head on the floor several times before I managed to turn on the flashlight. As luck would have it, Tim looked up and the beam of light blinded him momentarily. He loosened his grip on the man, who then made a run for the door and left the house.

The police arrived shortly after the intruder left. Their office was about 250 metres from our house and someone must have reported the commotion. They made sure we were all right and said they would find the man who had broken into our house in the morning. After they left, we started going down the hall and back to bed. Our flashlight was still on and we saw liquid on the floor. Tim figured it was blood. He said, "I know I hit the guy but I didn't realize just how hard." It was then that I looked at his back. There was blood all over it from the axe attack.

I guess we could have gone to the first aid clinic but they had no electricity either and only limited first aid material. I figured I could handle it. I remembered watching Westerns, where they poured alcohol on bullet wounds so I did the same thing with the cut. I then got some Elastoplast bandage material we had and attached it as best I could, and then we went back to bed. Nichola never woke up

The next day, the police arrived before we went to school. "We found him," they said, "in a village not far from here. He had Schweppes tonic water cans in their possession. You can't buy that kind here. Can you come and identify him?"

We went over to the police station. Four young men

were there. Tim recognized the intruder immediately and started to go after him, something he'd never done before or since. He was restrained by the police.

"Why did you do it?" Tim asked, "Why?"

The man didn't answer at the time but later we found out why. He was the older brother of one of our students. He had not been accepted to high school when he finished Grade 6. Since we had started the high school, many Grade 6 students who previously would not have gone to high school were going. He was angry at the system and Tim and I represented the system so he took it out on us.

When we moved to the Trobriand Islands, we were once again without transport for the first few months. Then one of the British volunteers in Alotau contacted us. "We are going back to England," he said, "and we need somebody to take our cat. If you take the cat, we'll give you our car." He went on to explain that although the car ran, it wouldn't go up any hills. Everyone in the town knew that and so no one would buy it. He also knew that there were no big hills where we lived and we had no vehicle. We agreed. A friend said he would give the car a tune-up and put it on the next barge coming out to the island. The cat arrived, a lovely ginger tom who was completely independent and only needed us for food and an occasional stroke. The car arrived a few weeks after the cat.

It was a white Mazda 929 station wagon, rusting but running. The students were just as excited as we were.

Everyone wanted to go for a ride. There had been trucks on the island for years but we don't think there had ever been a car with a back seat. We gave lots of people rides and then went home.

That evening we decided we would drive to the Kiriwina Lodge for supper. We arranged a babysitter and Tim and I left in our car for an evening out. The hotel was run by an Australian who was also the bank agent, the airline ticket agent, and the chairman of the school's Board of Governors. It was about 8km to the hotel and it was dark by the time we left the house. We had driven about 5km when there was a strange noise.

"Stop, Tim. There's something not right," I said, hoping I was wrong.

"There's no point in stopping here. We can't see anything. We might as well keep going to the hotel and someone can look at it there," Tim responded.

"Tim, the car feels wobbly," I replied, not knowing how else to describe the strange vibrations. Just after I said these words, the front tire on the passenger's side rolled away from the car, leaving us momentarily suspended on three wheels. Tim put his foot on the brake and as we slowed down, the car eventually tipped down to rest on the axle. The headlights of the car showed the tire disappearing across the road, down a gully, up the other side, and into some jungle. Tim passed me the flashlight.

"I'll get the tire," he said. "See if you can find the nuts." I bit back a sarcastic comment and dutifully got out of the lopsided car and proceeded to walk down the deserted road looking for wheel nuts. It was like looking for the proverbial needle in the haystack. Tim had the good job. A tire was easy to find, even in the dark. Eventually we decided we weren't ever going to find the nuts. The road was narrow and there was thick jungle on either side. The thought of looking for nuts in the jungle sent shivers down my spine. What other creepy crawlies could be there? Tim had the brilliant idea of taking a nut off each of the other tires and reattaching he fourth tire. All the other nuts were very loose so he tightened them as well. We never bothered getting any more nuts. Three seemed to work just as well as four and it made getting the tire off and on that much easier whenever we had a flat tire.

Eventually we found out that our friend had just finished putting on new brake pads when the call came to get the car down to the wharf right away. The barge was about to leave. When we picked up the car, we didn't think to check whether the nuts on the wheels needed tightening.

The car gave us a certain amount of prestige in the community and led to an unforgettable encounter.

Tim and I and Nichola were the only Europeans living in the community of Losuia, the district administrative headquarters. There was also the man who ran the hotel, the man and his employee who ran the trade store, the priest and one of the nuns at the mission station and a lady on the other side of the island who was trying to establish a resort. During our second year, a British volunteer teacher was sent out from England.

When the District Officer in Charge (DOIC) discovered that the New Zealand High Commissioner and his wife were coming on an official visit, he went to see Tim to ask if the car could be used to chauffeur them around the island. Tim agreed and was then asked to be the chauffeur.

The couple arrived on the Saturday morning plane and were due to depart on the Monday afternoon. Everyone went to the airstrip. The car had been polished and swept out. It was as clean as a car that age and vintage could be. Nichola and I sat in the front with Tim driving. When we arrived at the airstrip, everyone laughed and waved. Just before the plane arrived the DOIC went to see Tim.

"Your wife and child cannot ride with you in the car," he said. "It wouldn't be right. They can go back to Losuia in one of the trucks." His word was law and I was now going to be one of the cheering throngs, not one of the chosen. It was disappointing. The plane arrived. The New Zealand High Commissioner and his wife were easy to spot as they looked around anxiously hoping someone would greet them. The DOIC whisked them over to the trusty Mazda 929 and introduced them to the driver. Once the luggage arrived, Tim had to lift it over the back seat into the cargo area as the trunk of the car had refused to open for some time.

The New Zealand High Commissioner started to get into the front of the car. Tim explained that they were both expected to ride in the back. So he held the door open for them and they both graciously squeezed into the back seat.

As they drove towards town, they of course asked Tim why he was driving. He explained, "Our car was the only car with a back seat and air conditioning." As all the windows of the car were open and it was boiling hot, the New Zealand High Commissioner's wife asked about the air conditioning.

"If you lift the plywood your feet are resting on," Tim replied, "you'll find the air conditioning.

Saturday was mail day when we lived on the Trobriand Islands. If we wanted to read the mail on the day it arrived, Tim would get a ride and go out to the airport, get the mail bags, take them to the post office and sort the mail. The postmaster was quite happy to leave the mail in the bags until Monday morning and regular post office hours. We couldn't. The mail went out on Monday and if answers were needed, they had to be done on the weekend. In addition, we were mail dependent; it was our weekly link to the world we'd left behind.

Nichola was about one at the time and into everything. She had been up since dawn and by 9:30, I felt it was time for her father to take over. There was no power, no TV, and very few toys, so whatever entertainment and stimulation she got was from us.

Tim took the hint and said he'd take her to the airport to get the mail. "Stay here, relax, read a book, put your feet up. I'll take my turn when I get back."

I figured that I would have two hours of quiet. I made coffee and had just snuggled into my favourite corner with a book when I heard footsteps coming up the stairs.

The house was built on stilts and there was a cement staircase leading up to the back door.

Mispah, the woman who helped look after Nichola during the week, had brought over some ripe bananas. I thanked her and returned to my 'quiet' time. All of a sudden, there were footsteps running up the stairs.

"Quick, missus," Mispah said breathlessly, "there's snake going into your house."

I went outside with a sinking feeling in the pit of my stomach. Sure enough, a large snake, between two and three metres long, had curled itself around the sewer pipe and was going up into the house through the gap between the pipe and siding.

My quiet was shattered. Our house was about 200 metres from the police station and my first job was to get help. I ran over to the police station, which shared space with the post office and a small market area, and asked them for help.

Immediately, the three policemen on duty plus most of the island ran to my house. There must have been fifty people watching the bottom half of the snake trying to get through the hole. The top half had already made it.

The police officer in charge said, "We'll go into your house and see where the snake is."

I was in no position to argue and soon fifty people were in my bathroom trying to decide where the snake was because they couldn't see it. The eventual consensus was that the snake was between the siding on the outside and the interior bathroom walls. There was nothing for it, they'd have to rip out the bathroom wall.

As the fifty people left my house to go home and get

their tools, I found myself sitting at the table wondering what I'd done to deserve this. There was a knock on the door and Mispah's brother Peter was there. "I'll get the snake for you," he said.

I followed him outside and as I watched, he grabbed the tail of the snake just before it disappeared forever into the bowels of my house, and yanked. The whole snake fell out. He picked up a rock and killed it and left the carcass in our driveway.

Fifty people returned armed with the tools they felt were appropriate to ripping out the wall of my house and also killing a snake. They were disappointed to find out that the problem had been sorted. The excitement was gone from their day. Just as the last person left, and I returned to my book, Tim arrived home with Nichola.

"Did you have a nice quiet time?" he asked.

Tim hired Ernest Gowlei to help with the non-educational parts of running a school. He drove the truck, helped with repairs, provided us with local knowledge and guidance. His wife, Rose, was Nichola's babysitter. Mispah was Rose's sister who helped out periodically. Ernest had returned to the Trobs after years of working in Port Moresby. He was a qualified ground engineer and had worked at Jackson's Airport in Port Moresby. Tim asked him one day why he was working as a handyman, making a fraction of what he could make in the city, working for one of the airlines.

Ernest asked Tim why he worked. Tim replied, "To make money, I guess."

Ernest asked, "Why do you make money?"

Tim replied, "So I can buy food and the things we need."

Ernest then asked. "Once you have everything you need, then what?"

"I save the money for my old age," Tim suggested.

Ernest replied, "What do you want to do when you are old?"

Tim answered, "Sit on a white sandy beach and occasionally go fishing."

Ernest said, "Exactly. I can do that now."

7. 125 SIMPSON STREET, SAULT STE. MARIE, ONTARIO OCTOBER 1982-JANUARY 1983

We were still at Losuia when I became pregnant with our second child. The closest doctor was on the mainland. Because of the nature of Nichola's birth, he suggested that I should be close to a hospital for the last 6 weeks of my pregnancy. He and his wife invited me to stay with them in Alotau, about an hour's flight from Losuia. Tim and I went through the various options. All of them involved Nichola coming with me and the more I thought about it, the more I thought I'd like to be with my family. Six weeks with friends is a long time; six weeks with family can also be a long time but family members tend to be more honest and accepting.

I wrote to my parents, asking them if Nichola and I could stay while we waited for the baby. They very generously agreed. It would be a huge inconvenience for them but I think their minds worked differently from ours. They felt they wouldn't have to worry about what was happening halfway around the world.

I was a returning resident. Nichola was on my passport but she had been registered at the British Embassy in Papua New Guinea. There was no Canadian Embassy and as Tim was British, it seemed to make sense. She had a British birth certificate, not a Canadian one.

I knew we should have done something before we left to return to Canada but Losuia was so far from anything that we just didn't do it. Instead, I booked our tickets so that we would fly into Sault Ste Marie, Michigan. I figured that as my parents lived in Sault Ste Marie, Ontario, they would be able to help me with any immigration issues.

We left Papua New Guinea at the beginning of October 1982. It was about 6 weeks before my due date. Luckily, I didn't look very pregnant but I did have a note from the doctor in Alotau stating that it was safe for me to fly. Up until our trip, Nichola had only ever worn flip flops. She didn't have any shoes. We traced her feet on a piece of paper and arranged for a couple who came on a tour of the Trobs from Australia to buy her a pair of shoes. They came just before we left and Nichola proudly wore them to meet her grandparents. She was remarkably well-behaved for a two year old. Everything was new to her so it wasn't hard to keep her entertained. We flew on and off for two days without actually sleeping in a bed. By the time I met my parents, I was pretty tired.

Just as I planned, we had to clear customs and immigration at the US-Canadian border. I went inside with Nichola to fill in the forms. The immigration officer looked at the paper- work and said, "Your daughter does not have the right papers to reside in Canada."

I think he was going to say more but I interrupted

him. I picked Nichola up and sat her on his desk and said, "I am just too tired. Why don't you keep her and I will come back tomorrow after I have slept and straighten the whole thing out."

The poor immigration official quickly said, "That really won't be necessary. I just wanted to let you know that you need to file her citizenship forms as soon as you can."

When we arrived at my parents' house, my mother toured her around the house and showed her where she was going to sleep. My mother showed her the bathroom. The toilet was perhaps the best toy my mother could have provided. No one could have had more joy flushing and reflushing the toilet. We had to drag her out of the bathroom for supper.

My mother had cooked three steaks for that first supper, and cut a bit off each one for Nichola, thinking that cooking a whole steak for a two year old would be a waste. Nichola hoovered up the pieces and then spent the rest of the meal looking for more. I am not sure that we had ever had fresh meat on the Trobs.

Nichola adjusted quickly to life in Sault Ste Marie. She called my mother Bubu, a Kiriwinan word meaning 'elder person'. My mother loved being called Bubu, and went by that name with all 13 of her grandchildren. My mother had found a preschool to which I took Nichola every morning. In the afternoons, Nichola would nap and I would write to Tim. We knew that it would take at least two weeks for a letter to arrive, and then a further two weeks for a reply. He wanted to know how Nichola was adjusting, how my parents were adjusting, and when the baby would arrive.

Before we left Losuia, the Catholic Mission said they would be happy to take any messages for Tim. They had a SKED service, a short wave radio service that provided a daily scheduled time when all the mission stations would report to the mainland. News from the mainland would be reported out to the stations. And requests from the stations would be made back. It was a lifeline for the mission stations on remote islands.

The plan was for my father to telephone the Catholic Mission in Alotau on the mainland and let them know that the baby had arrived. They would then relay the message to Father Cunningham at Guseweta, about 15 kilometres from Losuia. Father Cunningham would get on his motorbike and deliver the message to Tim. I carefully copied out the number of the Catholic Mission as well as the international calling information and pinned it above the telephone at my parents' house.

Finally, the baby arrived on December 1st and the message relay began. My father called Alotau and the call was answered by Sister Helen, a nun from the Trobriand Islands who happened to be in Alotau. She was thrilled to be the one to pass on the message to Father Cunningham that afternoon. Father Cunningham got on his motorbike and rode as fast as he could on his Honda 70 to tell Tim.

Tim arrived in Sault Ste Marie when the baby was about three weeks old. Tim and I eventually decided on a name, Victoria Emma Clare.

8. AIYURA NATIONAL HIGH SCHOOL, KAINANTU, EASTERN HIGHLANDS PROVINCE JANUARY 1983 – DECEMBER 1983)

We returned to Papua New Guinea for one more year, this time in the Highlands. Nichola earned small amounts of money picking coffee beans with her babysitter. She learned to speak Tok Pigin and at one point was able to translate. My sister, Fiona, had arrived for a visit. Tim and I went to school, leaving Nichola and Victoria with the babysitter and Fiona. The babysitter put Victoria in a bilum (a string bag) and took Nichola's hand. Fiona asked, "Where are you going?" to the babysitter. She didn't speak any English. Nichola translated the question and waited for the response. "We're going to her house," said Nichola and left. My sister had no idea where they were going or what they were going to do but Nichola had every confidence that it was going to work out.

1983 Bala, a Grade 11 student with Victoria Photo
courtesy JT Goddard

Tim was in charge of the Expressive Arts Department and I taught in the English Department. The Summer Institute of Linguistics (SIL) was a 10 minute drive away. It was a small American community with people dedicated to translating the Bible into the 700 languages found in PNG. Linguists and their families were finically supported by their churches in the United States. There were a few families from Canada. We would often go to the weekly market there where foods like strawberries and English potatoes were available. SIL had a store that sold many American products which we were able to use.

One day a couple from Echo Bay, Ontario who were working at SIL contacted us out of the blue. They were supported by a church group and had gotten our names and location from my father who was the doctor for one of their mothers. The man had been a student in England and had heard great things about the evangelist Billy Graham. He and a friend decided to go and hear him preach in Wembly Stadium. It was packed and at the end of the service as they were leaving, member's of Billy Graham's Crusade approached people and asked them for their name and the church they normally attended. It took some time, but churches were contacted and told of people in their congregation who had been at Wembley and were obviously looking for a connection within their church. I don't know whether it made a different to everyone, but it certainly touched the man who told us the story.

1983 Nichola made the cover of a calendar that was released after we left the country Photo courtesy JT Goddard

9. 125 SIMPSON STREET, SAULT STE. MARIE, ONTARIO FEBRUARY 1984 – AUGUST 1984

Even though Nichola was born in Papua New Guinea, and we enjoyed our work and our lifestyle there, we recognized that both our children would never be Papua New Guineans. The urge to be back amongst our own families was strong. We eventually decided on Canada. Tim felt that as Canada was good enough for Karsh and Leonard Cohen, it was good enough for him, too.

Once he received his landed immigrant status, we arranged our trip back to Canada, stopping for Christmas in Sydney, Australia for one last warm Christmas. At the end of January 1984, we returned to Canada, planning to stay in Sault Ste Marie with my parents again while Tim and I figured out what we were going to do. We enrolled Nichola in her old preschool, which had moved into new premises at Etienne Brule Public School.

For two years, we had managed without electricity ad running water. By far, the most difficult was not having a reliable source of water. In the early days on Trobs, I got up early one morning with Nichola, who had made a mess with the contents of her diaper. I picked her up and carried her down to the sea to wash her off. I returned to the house crying, telling Tim that I wasn't strong enough for this. Tim consoled me and then said we had to get ready to go to work. There was absolutely nothing else we could do.

A few years later, living with my parents while we were considering moving up North, Tim asked me what the most important criteria of moving there were. I said that I could handle most things if I had running water.

(Later, the list was amended to included electricity and a road. Then I learned that I had to be more specific. I wanted to live in a place that had a road that went somewhere, not just around the community.)

Tim rented office space in downtown Sault Ste Marie and set himself up as a writer/ photographer. Over time, he got a few contracts but not enough to support me and the girls. Tim began applying for teaching jobs across Canada. We were asleep one night when my father pounded on the bedroom door. "Tim! Wake up! There's a man on the phone for you. It's about a job!"

Sure enough, the man on the phone wanted us both to come to Prince Albert, Saskatchewan to interview for teaching jobs in Black Lake, Saskatchewan. We found an old school atlas that showed Prince Albert and Lake Athabasca. The caller said that Black Lake was between those two points.

We registered with Unemployment Canada and they

subsidized our flight to Saskatoon. We then took a bus to Prince Albert. We were interviewed separately by Chief and Council and the man who had called us. When the dust settled, Tim had the principal's job and I was going to teach Grade 3.

10. Black Lake First Nation, Black Lake, Saskatchewan (August 1984 -June 1987)

B lack Lake, Saskatchewan was a Dene community about 60 km south of the Northwest Territories. It was a fly-in community with no roads connecting it to the rest of Canada. Tim drove a UHaul to Saskatoon and the girls and I flew and met him there. Indian Affairs had chartered a plane to take teachers and their families to the small town of Stony Rapids. From there, one group went in smaller floatplanes to Fond du Lac, and the rest of us went to Black Lake in a variety of vehicles. The girls and I sat in the front of a truck while Tim and the rest of the staff got to ride in the back of the closed-sided vehicle. There were no windows and for 16 long kilometres, they had no idea where they were.

Our time in Papua New Guinea had served us well and we came prepared with food, bedding and cooking utensils in our luggage. By the time we arrived in Black Lake, the store was closed and we ended up feeding the rest of the staff who weren't so prepared. It didn't take long to settle in to our new life. Nichola was old enough to go to the afternoon junior kindergarten. Victoria stayed with the babysitter. It was hard to imagine a place more different than Papua New Guinea, but we liked the North and its people.

1984 Principal's house, Black Lake

School ended for the Christmas holidays and we decided that we would stay in Black Lake. Tim and I didn't want the girls to get over-excited about Christmas. We didn't have a television and Nichola couldn't read— she was only 4. The Hudson Bay store had a few Christmas decorations but the girls didn't come with me when I went shopping. Nichola knew about Christmas but had no idea when Christmas Day was. We had ordered Christmas presents from Sears and our families had sent gifts but they all arrived by mail and were delivered to the school. We left them there.

On Christmas Eve, we put the girls to bed. Tim picked up the gifts and brought them home. I began wrapping as he went out on the skidoo and cut down a tree by the light of the snowmobile. Christmas was ready by 11 pm. We filled the girls' stockings and laid them on their beds.

The girls woke up at their normal time and came into our room. "Guess what?" I said. "Today is Christmas!"

We had a lovely day. No one was tired or cranky. Tim and I were the only ones that noticed that it was minus 50 degrees Celsius. Exactly one year before, we had spent Christmas Day in Sydney, Australia on the beach.

The cold was fierce at Black Lake. We adjusted, sort of. In February, Tim as principal, sent staff home early at lunchtime. The water was going to be shut off for several days and we were told to collect as much as we could for cooking and cleaning. The alternative would be getting water from the lake. I went home and filled the bathtub first, thinking we could use the water for washing the girls and flushing the toilet.

Once it was filled, Nichola asked, "Can Victoria and I play in the water?" I agreed they could.

I had forgotten that we had a 3 month old St Bernard puppy called Winston. Nichola, of course, encouraged the dog to jump into the bathtub with them. I heard the splashing and found the three of them having a great time but making a watery mess on the floor. I took the dog and dragged him to basement and shut the door behind him, figuring he could dry off there. He began to whine and scratch and bark. I ignored it and began making lunch. Nichola heard the noise and couldn't stand to hear the dog crying so she opened the basement door and the dog raced back to the bathroom and jumped back into the tub. I grabbed Winston again but this time I put him out the front door. I then cleaned up the water, got the girls out of the tub and dressed and then got lunch on the table.

Tim arrived home and asked, "What's that lump of ice on the front porch?" I realized that it was the dog. Because it was so cold, he had pretty well frozen to one spot. We managed to free him from the ice and brought him inside and warmed him up. He recovered, but never went near the bathtub again.

It had been minus 40 degrees Celsius for weeks on end and we had all gotten used to it. It suddenly warmed up one day to about zero and as Tim and I walked home for lunch, we found Nichola and Victoria in bathing suits on the steps leading up to the house. They thought spring had arrived.

Because Black Lake was a fly-in community, the fresh food arrived once a week on the same plane as the mail. Whenever anyone went south, they took with them lists of shopping. For a few weeks, the newly appointed director of education lived with us as his house was not ready. He had been down south for meetings and on his return, he decided to make us dinner with special ingredients he had brought back from Prince Albert. Bill took over our kitchen on a Saturday and told us to go for a walk and come back at supper time. We did as he asked and on our return could smell the most wonderful aromas. We sat at the table and Bill served us spaghetti alfredo which we had never had before. It was delicious and Bill had spent all afternoon making it. Nichola finished her pasta quickly, and turned to Bill and asked, "Can I have more Kraft dinner, please?"

Both Nichola and Victoria began their formal education at Black Lake where the language of the playground in those days was Dene. There was no television in our first year and we relied on getting books from mail order places in England and Canada. Tim began reading *The Hobbit* to Nichola, a few pages a night. I was never allowed to read it to her because I couldn't do the voices properly. Nichola began afternoon kindergarten in September 1984. Within a few weeks, she was completely at home. Eventually, the basement became the girls' playground, especially when it got cold. All the girls had to do was open the door and go outside to be immediately surrounded by children who wanted to play with them.

There was sand everywhere in the community and play was pretty rough and tumble. The girls took countless utensils outside to dig in the sand which they always lost. From the three years we were there, I am convinced there is a place settling for 6 people that anthropologists will find in years to come.

It's funny the things you worry about as a parent. In Black Lake, I worried about fire. In those days, if a house caught on fire, it just burned to the ground as there was no fire department. The first house I saw burn to the ground was because of children playing with matches. When another house caught on fire for the same reason, I went home and took Nichola and Victoria to the fire. Within 15 minutes there was nothing left. All you could see was a metal bed frame, and the remains of a fridge and a stove. I remember telling them that this is what happens when you play with matches. Nichola told me much later that she was 18 before she struck her first match.

Over time, both Nichola and Victoria learned Dene, and participated in the life of the community. They lined up to get money on Treaty Day from Indians Affairs.

They were rejected but that didn't stop them participating.

*Treaty Day, Black Lake, 1986 Victoria and Nichola
sitting on the knee of one of the RCMP officers; Chief
Danny Robillard is on the right*

Black Lake was also a Catholic community and when a nun arrived in the community to take the Grade 1s for First Communion classes, Nichola went with them. I walked by her Grade 2 classroom one day and saw her standing with the other students saying, "I am a Chipewyan Indian." The girls ate dried meat, both caribou and moose, made by the women of the community, and liked it best with Tenderflake lard and bannock.

I taught Grade 3 for a year. We struggled to find babysitters for the morning. Tim and I used to argue about whose job was more important. He had a whole school to supervise and I had a group of unruly Grade 3s. I usually lost the argument and stayed home until the babysitter arrived. Ultimately, it was the push I needed to get into curriculum development. In our second year, I began working on what Tim named a Community Related Integrated Studies Program (CRISP). The theory behind the program was that the students would Learn English much faster if the material was familiar to them.

Rather than reading *A Duck is a Duck*, a reader developed for schools in southern Canada, the students would read stories about their community. By the time we left in June 1987, a curriculum was in place for Kindergarten–Grade 6.

When we left Black Lake in June 1987, both girls had skills those living in an urban setting might not have. They could speak and understand the Dene language. They knew the difference between a ptarmigan and a spruce grouse. They could bait a fish hook and clean a fish. They didn't know any television shows but could do 'Layer Cake' on the computer. They could amuse themselves for hours building forts, playing school, and on one memorable occasion, hairdresser. However, they could not ride a bicycle or jump rope. They had not been a Spark or a Brownie, nor taken swimming or piano lessons.

11. Shields Townsite, Dundurn, Saskatchewan June 1987 – August 1989

We arrived in Shields Townsite, near Dundurn, Saskatchewan, in June 1987. Tim was returning to the University of Saskatchewan in Saskatoon for a year to complete his B.Ed. Shields was close to Blackstrap Mountain, 'the pimple on the prairie' built in the early 1970s for the Canada Winter Games. It was the only high ground: the rest was prairies, a great contrast to the boreal forest of northern Saskatchewan. We moved into an unfurnished house and for the first time in our married life, had to buy furniture.

House in Shields, near Dundurn, Saskatchewan

Saskatoon was 40 minutes away and had a lot of second-hand furniture stores. After we bought bunk beds for the girls, an L-shaped couch and a dining room table and chairs and arranged for their delivery, we decided that we would buy ourselves a new bed. We had always slept on mattresses other people had used. We went to Sears. For some reason the mattresses were in full view of the escalator. The salesman encouraged us to lie on them and try them out. It was incredibly embarrassing. The mattresses were expensive and as we dithered, I remembered something.

We hadn't been married very long when I stumbled across an advertisement in *The Post Courier*, Papua New Guinea's national newspaper, for waterbeds. Apparently, or according to the ads, they were great in tropical climates. There were three sizes, twin, queen, and king. I mentioned it to Tim and he thought it was a great idea and that we should get a king sized one so there would be lots of room. I ordered it and great was the excitement the day it came. It wasn't a very big package and as another teacher pointed out, we'd need a frame to supported the mattress when it was full of water.

There was a handyman at school so we gave him the measurements. The frame arrived and we realized that the bed was too big for our bedroom. When we moved to our next posting, we took the waterbed, still in its original package, and the frame. The bedroom was big enough but we didn't have running water the whole time we were there. Our last place in PNG had running water and a big enough room. On our arrival we were told that waterbeds were not allowed because of the constant shaking of the houses from earthquakes. At the end of our time in PNG I sold the waterbed, still in its original package, and the frame.

The first jobs we had in Canada included furnished housing but when we moved into that empty house in Shields, the time had come to revisit my hope of a waterbed. We found one, complete with frame that we knew would fit in our bedroom. The store only delivered outside of Saskatoon once a month and we had just missed the delivery. Tim and I slept on the floor for another three weeks. We had a call from the store confirming delivery the next morning. When the truck arrived, I told Tim that I would keep the girls busy while he put the bed together. He carried the wood and the bladder—I now knew the technical term for the mattress —up the stairs. I had been sleeping on the floor for 6 weeks at this point and was fantasizing what a bed would feel like, when Tim came back downstairs. "I hate to burst your bubble," he said, "but the 4 pieces of wood are 4 different lengths. They won't fit together."

We phoned the store and explained the situation to the manager. He said he would come out with new bed boards just as soon as he could get them. He apologized and promised to put them together for us. We waited and about two hours later the manager and another fellow arrived. True to their word, they put the frame together for us. They came downstairs and said, "It's all set now. All you have to do is put in the bladder and the heater and fill it. Remember, it will take some time to warm up." With those words, they left.

Tim went upstairs, got the bladder and the heater out

of the box and in the wooden frame and connected the hose that ran from the outside tap, up the wall to the second floor window, to the bed. With great ceremony, we turned on the tap and the bladder slowly began filling. Tim came downstairs, had coffee, went back upstairs to check on things. He came back down. "It's going to take a while to fill," he pronounced. So, we got on with our lives.Another hour passed. Victoria who would have been four at the time, shrieked, "Winston is drinking the water." Winston was our full grown St Bernard. We both shot upstairs and found that Winston had climbed (or jumped) onto the bladder, the pressure forcing the hose to detach. The hose was filling up the cracks in the bladder on the outside and he was happily drinking any water that came his way. It took us quite some time to restore order. At that point, the bladder was about ½ full. I noticed that the heating pad was on the top of the bladder. I mentioned it to Tim. "Is the heating pad in the right place?" I asked, "Shouldn't it be underneath the bladder?"

Tim saw what I meant, and said, "You know what this means—we're going to have to pull back the bladder, put the heating pad underneath and then drop the bladder on top." We had to get the girls as it took both Tim and I all our strength to pull back the bladder. One of the girls dropped it in place and we were good to go, or so we thought.

The heating pad had a cord and the cord was short and would only work if it could go through the frame to the closest socket. We didn't have a drill so we had to borrow a drill. Eventually, we got all the pieces together and we were able to sleep on it that night. In retrospect, it probably would have been easier to just get a mattress.

Tim left for the university before the girls went to school. He explained to me that he wanted to treat going to university like a job. I found out some time later that like any job it began with coffee and *The Globe and Mail* at a Tim Horton's near the university.

In the fall of 1987 I was hired by the Saskatchewan Ski Association to develop and run a cross country ski program. Two instructors were sent into different schools across the province to introduce cross country skiing to students in Grades 4-6. Initially, I had an office in Saskatoon but after a few months it was moved to our house. It meant I was there to meet the girls after school.

In a way, the two years in Dundurn introduced the girls to mainstream Canada. They took swimming lessons, learned how to skip, and after much help mastered the art of riding a two wheeler. They both took figure skating lessons though as much as they wanted to skate for Canada, neither of them was very good.

The girls would catch the bus at about 7.45 am in the morning and return home around 4:00 pm. I would have a snack ready because I had learned that the girls were much happier having eaten something. We'd settle in to watch "Three's Company" and "Silver Spoons" on TV. At 5 pm, I turned off the TV and began making supper. The girls could use that time however they wished.

Tim would arrive home between 5 pm and 6 pm and

ask if the girls had done their homework. I usually said I had no idea.

Tim felt that I should be more involved than I was. He said several times, "The minute the girls get off the bus, they should do their homework. Then, they can play, watch TV, do whatever they want."

I replied, "My mother never made us do homework, she just expected us to do it. She said if the school ever called her and said we hadn't done our homework, she would get involved. I don't remember that ever happening. That," I said to Tim, "is what I want the girls to learn. It is not my responsibility to make them do their homework. It's theirs. I don't want it to be mine. I don't want to spend the next 20 years supervising homework, do you?"

We agreed to use my method until it was shown not to work. There were a couple of incidents where Nichola had to set the alarm to get up early to finish something but no one ever phoned to say the girls had not done their homework. We would help if asked, but otherwise, let them do it on their own. My method worked all the way through elementary and high school.

Tim's academic career took off. He was awarded a scholarship and asked to stay at the University of Saskatchewan for a second year to complete the master's program in educational administration. I think he would have enjoyed educational philosophy more but he needed to go into an area where there were jobs. I extended my work with Sask Ski for another year. We managed with some financial help from our parents.

By March of 1989 I could no longer hide the fact that

I was pregnant from Nichola and Victoria. Neither Tim nor I were very good explaining the facts of life so we were extremely uncomfortable sharing the news. Victoria at 6 ½ had heard on the playground about someone losing a baby. We reassured her that our baby was fine. All Nichola could say over and over again was, "I don't believe it, I just don't believe it." She did come round in time, though neither girl was very impressed with the makeshift babysitters that spring.

Tim accepted a position as principal of Attagoyuk School in Pangnirtung on Baffin Island in April. We then had to prepare our sealift order. The school board advanced money so that new teachers could get dry goods and frozen meats and vegetables for the year because of the high prices in the shops in Pang where a stalk of celery cost $9 and a 4 litre pail of ice cream was $28.

The lists of food came to us in French and we did our best but ended up with a few things we never used, including some tinned hot dogs—a crate of twelve boxes of twelve tins of hot dogs! I am not sure what we thought we were buying. We also had to include a crib and baby food with our order. We didn't order any formula because I was going to breast feed.

Kate was born on July 18th in Saskatoon. Tim picked me up from the hospital on one of the hottest days of the summer in a car that wasn't air-conditioned. For some reason that has eluded me to this day, he had to stop at one of the supermarkets to buy oven gloves. Kate and I were pretty hot and bothered by the time he came out.

I ended up going back into hospital with a DVT, leaving Tim with the two girls and a baby to pack the house by the beginning of August when we were flying east. I never went back to the house and went from the hospital to the airport. We all flew to Toronto together. We separated there. Tim and the girls flew to Ottawa and then Pangnirtung where they met Tim's mother who had come to Canada to unpack and settle the girls into their new community. Kate and I were met by a friend who helped get us on the plane to Sault Ste. Marie where once again, my parents helped us out.

Tim's mother Betty took great delight in opening up the boxes and storing everything in its rightful place. One box arrived labeled 'Top of fridge'. I think in a desperate move to finish packing, Tim just ran his arm across the top of the fridge and everything that was there fell into a box.

All our great plans fell apart. I wasn't able to breast feed the baby because of the drugs I was on and we hadn't shipped any formula. I didn't get to Pangnirtung until Thanksgiving. Betty had to leave the week before I arrived but I managed to figure out her system.

12. Pangnirtung, Nunavut
August 1989 – June 1990

It was not one of our better moves. All the activities that Nichola and Victoria had enjoyed in Dundurn were not available in Pang. There were no trees, lots of ice, not much snow, and it was cold and dark between November and February. We thought that the girls would have no trouble adjusting because of the other places they had lived. The girls worked hard at trying to make friends, inviting classmates over to the house, but adults were wary of newcomers, and their children picked up the feeling. Nichola asked us one day, "Why can't I make friends here?" It was difficult to explain to a 10 year old.

I was able to find some curriculum work while we were there. Using the CRISP principle, I developed language material for an RCMP Special Constable as well as a woman who worked in the print shop. I worked at home on the materials in the morning developing vocabulary lists and language exercises based on the office forms from their employers. In the afternoon, the two students would come twice a week on different days. In many ways, it was the perfect job. I didn't need a babysitter and I was at home when the girls finished school. It seemed to go well. Arctic College presented the material at a circum-polar conference later in the year.

On a glorious spring day, Tim and Nichola went for a dog sled ride with a friend from Pangnirtung. The ice was still in the fjord, although cracks were appearing. Tim was excited to take some action shots that would make him the envy of photographers everywhere. Both Nichola and Tim travelled in the *komatiq*, the sled pulled by the dogs. The driver stood on the back of the sled, alternating running and riding. The dogs ran in a fan formation while they were on the ice. In Black Lake, when the dogs were on land, they ran in pairs, or single file through the woods.

About 2 hours from the community, they stopped for a break. There was a crack in the ice about a foot wide and Tim thought if he jumped across the crack and lay on the ice, he could get a great photograph of the dogs pulling the sled across the ice. He jumped across the crack — but the ice gave way and he went into the Arctic Ocean. He was wearing Sorel boots, a parka, and snow pants and they immediately filled with water. Quick as a flash, the driver jumped off the sled and reached Tim just before he disappeared under the ice.

To this day, we have no idea how he managed to get Tim out of the water and onto the ice. All Nichola could do was watch. Tim ended up taking off all his outer wet clothes and Nichola snuggled in beside him in the sled, under a blanket, trying to prevent him from getting hypothermia. As soon as they arrived back at the house,

Tim got in the bathtub, gradually warming up the temperature of the water as he thawed out. It was a pivotal moment in Nichola's life. I don't think she ever wanted to feel that helpless again.

My father once told me that sometimes in life you make a mistake. The thing to do is to admit the mistake and move on. Tim and I admitted that the move to Pangnirtung was a mistake and at the end of the school year, we packed up and took the three girls, and Winston, the aging St Bernard dog, to La Ronge, Saskatchewan. La Ronge was halfway between Black Lake and Dundurn, nearly at the end of the road. I'd made Tim promise that anywhere we moved to after Pangnirtung had to have running water, electricity, and a road going somewhere.

13. QUANDT CRESCENT, LA RONGE, SASKATCHEWAN AUGUST 1990 – AUGUST 1993

Tim was hired as the Superintendent of Education for the Lac La Ronge Indian Band. It was a challenging job with schools in seven communities. We bought an Izuzu Trooper with 4wheel drive which meant he could visit all the schools, in most kinds of weather.

Tim and I bought our first house in La Ronge and we were finally able to get everything out of storage and out of my parents' attic. Nichola started Grade 5 at Pre-Cam School and finished Grade 7 at Churchill High School by the time we left three years later. Victoria went into Grade 3 and Kate was still at home.

1990 Spring in La Ronge l-r: Kate, Victoria, Nichola

I had taken the girls out cross-country skiing when we lived in Dundurn but although we had taken the skis with us to Pang, the ice made any cross-country skiing challenging. La Ronge had fabulous trails at Nut Point that we walked for three seasons and skied in the winter. Nichola took to it like a duck to water and in her last year in La Ronge began racing competitively.

La Ronge had the first library the girls could access independently and quickly learned how the system worked and the joys of interlibrary loans. Tim had introduced them to the fantasy world of Tolkien's *The Hobbit* and later, *Lord of the Rings* and they explored other fantasy writers. When a new David Eddings arrived in their name, Nichola would volunteer to do the dishes so Victoria could finish the book quickly and lend it to Nichola. Victoria read faster but Nichola liked having the book longer so she could read it over again immediately. Both girls felt they had the best of the deal.

Sadly, Winston started getting cranky in his old age and bit a visitor to the house. Tim felt we had no option but to take him to the vet. It was quiet in the house without a dog, and we decided to get another one.

There was a dental hygienist at the girls' school and at some point during their first year Nichola talked to her about the gap between her two front teeth. The dental hygienist called us, explaining that she had referred her to an orthodontist. His office was in Prince Albert, a three hour trip each way. The orthodontist felt he could close the gap, and thus began our monthly trips to Prince Albert (PA), sometimes travelling six hours for a 5 minute appointment.

It was during one of those trips that Nichola and I decided to surprise everyone by getting a puppy at the Humane Society in PA. It wasn't just the puppy, we had to buy all the things a puppy needs. That was an expensive trip. We arrived back home and I went in first to tell Tim and the girls that Nichola had a surprise for them.

Tim said, "No, wait. I have a surprise as well."

Victoria came round the corner carrying a puppy called Petra that Tim had been given at work. Nichola entered the house carrying Charlie, the pound puppy. It seemed to take a long time to train the puppies and there were always messes to clean up. One of the dogs actually carried in frozen poo to nibble on during the day, fondly remembered as the poopscicle.

The girls were also able to join Girl Guides again and I was able to help as a leader. The provincial Girl Guide organization sent a trainer to La Ronge to help with program details. Her mother-in-law had been the Queen's Guider, and she talked about the establishment of traditions within families. Every Christmas she and her husband and three girls would make a picnic and head into the woods, decorate a tree for the birds, have a winter picnic and cut down a Christmas tree and bring it home.

I thought this sounded like a great tradition that we could begin, especially in La Ronge where everyone just went off in the bush to get their tree. I mentioned the idea to Tim and he reluctantly agreed. In previous years, Tim had taken the older two girls and the tree had always fit in the back of the Izuzu Trooper when part of the back seat was laid flat.

With Kate and I now coming, there he wasn't sure

how everyone would fit with the tree. I was one step ahead of him. I knew of 30 m of extension cord in the garage from the electric lawn mower that I ran over in the summer. I suggested that we could use it to tie the tree onto the roof of the car.

The morning of the Christmas tree/picnic/ bird feeding was freezing. It was minus 40 C without the wind chill. Tim wisely suggested that all we could do was get the tree. The picnic and feeding the birds was not going to happen. So, we all piled into the car and drove about 5 km out of town. We stopped and all got out. The trees were pretty well picked over so we all got back in the car and drove about 20 km up the highway and went on a side road for about a kilometre till we could go no further. We all got out. Tim led the way, carrying the axe over his shoulder. Nichola was behind him, then Victoria, and then Kate and me.

Within 5 minutes Kate was crying because she was so cold. I got the keys from Tim and took her back to the car to warm up. Three minutes later, Victoria arrived, crying as well. "I picked a tree and Dad said it was no good," she sobbed.

Five minutes later, Nichola arrived, crying with tears of frustration. "Dad just won't listen. He just wants to pick what he wants."

Now there were three sobbing children on the back seat. Tim arrived, dragging a tree and carrying the axe. He was furious that the girls had deserted him. He threw the tree on the roof. "Open the windows," he demanded. We all opened them. He started to thread the yellow extension cord around the tree and through the windows.

"Pull it tight," he instructed, and we all pulled down on the cord.

"Now tie a knot," he said. So, I tied a knot. Then, he tried to open the driver's door, and it wouldn't open. We had to loosen the cord so the doors would open and Tim could get in the driver's seat. We drove to the highway and started the drive back to the house.

"Tim," I said, "The tree is slipping."

"No, it isn't," he growled.

"The top of the tree is touching the high- way," I said.

He pulled the car over to the side and said, "You drive!"

I crawled into the driver's seat.

Meanwhile, Tim climbed onto the hood of the car and pulled the tree back up by the trunk. He then got back in the passenger's side and told everyone to pull on the yellow cord as hard as they could. He tied a huge knot and pulled on the cord as we drove back to town. We pulled into the driveway and tried to undo the cord so we could get out of the car. Unfortunately, driving for half an hour in minus 40 degree temperatures meant that the extension cord was completely frozen. We all had to climb out the windows. Tim ended up borrowing bolt cutters from our neighbours to cut the cord.

To top it all off, the tree was too tall for the living room, and Tim had to chop the top off so we ended up with a squat Christmas tree. People came in, looked at the trunk, and went out to see whether the top was coming through the roof. By the time the next Christmas rolled around, we were living in Edmonton, and we just picked a tree up at the mall. It was so much easier.

I spent one of the years in La Ronge finishing my BEd. I also had an epiphany workwise. I had spent years trying to prove that women could have it all. I was sitting in a waiting room reading the free *Reader's Digest*. One of the articles described the author's childhood as miserable. His parents constantly fought over who had to stay at home with which ever child was sick. His mother was chronically tired as most of the housework fell to her. His father never came home early to help. The author felt his childhood was miserable.

I didn't want to be that person. I started looking for part time work and I was usually home when the girls came home from school. I realized I couldn't have it all but that it didn't matter. Tim had the career and I had a succession of interesting jobs. I ended up working for the local newspaper for the last year we were in La Ronge. The hours were flexible and the work fascinating.

Towards the end of our time in La Ronge I was asked to take some Saskatchewan Education materials north to a family with six children who were using correspondence courses to complete their education. They gave me the materials and told me that the float plane was chartered and would leave the next day. I got to the dock and the pilot stowed the material in the back of the plane. He and I the got in the front, he gave me a set of headphones showing me how to use them. We took off and climbed a little. I could see lakes and trees and rocks. After about an hour we landed on the water and taxied towards a small dock.

The entire family met us and carried all the material up to the house. I think the father was an American draft dodger who had met up with a Cree woman and built a place in the bush for their family. They had chickens and dogs and a cat. There was also a greenhouse which seemed to grow some interesting plants. The house consisted of 4 rooms : a living room/ dining room/ kitchen, a bedroom for the parents, a boys' bedroom and a girls' bedroom. The oldest girl was just finishing high school. Her father told me he had signed her up for Athabasca University correspondence courses. He believed that she would meet and marry someone in the area. She would never have to live in a town. The other children would follow the same path.

I went through the material with them and then returned to the plane. We flew back to La Ronge, landing just before dark, the pontoons just kissed the water. It is 30 years since I did that trip and I often wonder what happened to the family.

14. EDMONTON, ALBERTA
1993 -1995

After three years as superintendent, Tim wanted to get involved in the actual training of teachers. He was accepted into the PhD program in Educational Administration at the University of Alberta in Edmonton. We sold the house, rented another UHaul, and moved to rental accommodation in an area chosen for its schools. I told him I was good for two years but after that, he'd have to find a job. He had a funded position at U of A the first year. He was awarded a Killam Scholarship the second.

Tim and the girls lived in Edmonton but for the first 18 months, I spent two weeks in Edmonton, and then two weeks up north in fly-in communities. I would fly into Stoney Rapids, Saskatchewan on the east end of Lake Athabasca and check into the local hotel. Every day I would travel about 15 km to Black Lake and work with the teacher associates. On Friday I would return to the Stoney Rapids Hotel for the weekend and then fly to

Fond du Lac, a community about 75 km west in a plane that was small enough to land on the dirt strip.

I went up in late November for my last trip. Black Lake went well and on Monday morning I flew to Fond du Lac. I began teaching when I arrived. On Tuesday morning, there was a problem. One of the participant's brothers had flown to his trapline earlier in the fall using a chartered float plane. He would live in his cabin, set his traps, and then check them. He would skin any animals he caught and then bring the furs into The Bay store in Fond du Lac by skidoo in time for Christmas. His only way of communicating was with his radio phone. A call had come to his sister the previous evening, asking for help. He had been attacked by a black bear and wanted someone to come because he had been injured.

It was the 'in-between season'. There was too much ice for a float plane to land and the ice was not thick enough to support a plane on skis. The only way he could be reached was by helicopter and the closest helicopter was based in Prince Albert. The people in charge of wildlife got involved because they were concerned that a black bear had attacked the fellow. According to them, that rarely happened unless the bear was provoked or had rabies. There had been no reports of rabies but the officials were worried enough to get involved.

There was a new nurse at the Stoney Rapids clinic who had only been there for a day and she was asked to go in the helicopter to assess the fellow who had been attacked, treat him, and if necessary, bring him back to Stoney. When the wildlife people heard there was a helicopter flying in, they went to see the nurse. They gave her a machete and asked her to get the bear's head and bring it back so they could send samples to the provincial lab to check for rabies.

The helicopter arrived and the nurse got in beside the pilot, holding the machete. Her medical bag was placed behind the seat. The injured man met the helicopter when it landed. He had had on a heavy parka when the bear took a swipe at him. He had a few shallow gashes. She gave him a tetanus shot, bandaged his arm, and then reluctantly asked where the bear was.

He said, "I don't know. It ran away after I shot it."

The nurse collected her things, got back on the helicopter, still clutching the machete. When she arrived in Stoney Rapids, she packed up her things and left on the next available flight.

Eventually, I had taught just about every teacher assistant in northern Saskatchewan. By January of 1995, I began to look for work in and around Edmonton. The first job that was offered was as a teacher at the Edmonton Institution, a maximum security federal penitentiary known as The Max, located in northeastern Edmonton. It was about a 40 minute drive from where we lived but there was another teacher who lived close by and we were able to car pool.

My job was initially to be a substitute teacher, working both in the classroom as well as with individuals whose English was not their first language. Each day when I arrived, we were each given an emergency radio pager that we attached to our belts. We were told that if we felt there was a fight we couldn't separate or if things went out of control, we were to push the button. They told us, "It will take 3 or 4 minutes for the guards to respond—they won't run as it would cause pandemonium." Three minutes is a long time when you are waiting for help.

The inmates each got an allowance for coming to school. It gave them money for cigarettes and other supplies from the canteen. We were told to deduct money from them if they weren't working. They were all supposed to be doing correspondence courses. Most of them spent their time designing tattoos. There were three teachers and none of us ever deducted pay. As long as there was no trouble, we were happy.

The other two teachers had only recently qualified. Although I was the newest on the job, I had actually years more experience, albeit in a more mainstream school. The inmates at the Max were there because their punishment was over two years and of a serious enough nature that they had to be in a secure facility. My mother asked me one day if I had met any nice people. I reminded her where I was working.

The other teachers had arranged for a pizza and video afternoon. The male teacher went out to get the pizza and during the lunch break the other teacher was responsible for renting the video. Twenty-five inmates arrived to eat pizza, drink pop, and watch the video. It was a title I had never heard of, called *Natural Born Killers*. Needless to say, as the murdering duo began their killing spree in a prison, I sat watching the movie with my hand on the emergency radio pager, ready to hit it at the first sign of trouble.

I asked the teacher why this movie and she said, "It

was what they wanted to watch." I asked her if she had previewed it. She said she hadn't. The movie seemed to go on forever and I sat there, waiting for something to happen. Nothing did but when I arrived home, there was a call from the Sahtu Board of Education, asking me if I was still interested in a job I had applied for previously. I leapt at the chance.

I was offered a four month contract with the Sahtu Board of Education, based in Norman Wells, about halfway between Yellowknife and Inuvik, on the shores of the MacKenzie River. My contract was from the beginning of March until the end of June. I would rent an apartment in a government building which was close enough to walk to the regional office. A lot of my time would be spent in the smaller communities of the Sahtu as I looked into the feasibility of a teacher training program for teacher associates.

It couldn't have come at a better time. Tim was due to finish his PhD in June, the girls were all in school full-time, and after my time working in the jail, I was grateful that I had other work. Tim drove me to the airport with my luggage, my four Rubbermaid containers and my cross country skis. I was met in Norman Wells by the Director of Education who took me to my furnished apartment on the 2nd floor of a government housing complex. Between us, we managed to get everything upstairs. There was no elevator.

Tim and I had decided that I wouldn't get a phone. It was 1995, the internet was in its infancy and cell phones were big, bulky and expensive. I would use the internet and call from the office every Friday afternoon. By the time the contract ended, Tim would have finished his PhD and would be gainfully employed.

I settled into my new life quite easily. I had no responsibilities for anyone except myself. The director encouraged me to go to several of the communities that made up the Board to chat to community members to get an idea of what each community needed and wanted. I was back in the office at the end of the second week. I talked to Tim. Our oldest daughter, Nichola, was in a cross country ski race in Kananaskis country. He asked me if I needed the name of the hotel where they would be staying. I said, "No," I replied. "I'll call on Monday when I get to the office. I won't be near a phone over the weekend."

I had made arrangements with the office accountant to make a video of where I lived and worked for the girls and Tim. She would come over on Saturday morning with her camera and between us we would create something. I had put on new hiking boots and decided to carry the garbage down the stairs and out to the main bins outside. I stumbled on one of the stairs and heard my leg break as I made a grab for the bannister.

I tried shouting for help but then realized that the steel doors at each level prevented sound from carrying. I held my leg and bummed my way down the stairs and across the floor and then kicked the door again and again until somebody finally answered. It just happened to be a woman I had met the day before. She immediately sprang into action and called 911, forgetting of course, that 911 was not available in Norman Wells. Eventually, she got through to the Nursing Station who sent one of the hotel's vans that doubled as the ambulance. Once I got to the Nursing Station, an Xray confirmed that my leg was broken in five places. I needed the services of an orthopedic surgeon. The closest hospital was in Inuvik but the closest orthopedic surgeon was in Yellowknife. He was going on vacation and suggested that I be taken to Edmonton.

The nurses asked if they could let my husband know about the accident. Of course, I had no idea where Tim was staying and there wasn't anything he could do in any case. The nurses spoke to my father who spent the next two days trying to get in touch with Tim. I flew to Edmonton where they operated on my leg and eventually Tim got the nine messages my father had left on the answering machine on Sunday evening.

I returned to the house a few days later, and traveled north again once I could manage the stairs on a plane. I adjusted to life on crutches and the board organized a ride for me every morning and evening so I could get to and from work. Once a week, someone would take me shopping and I was able to wash my clothes in the bathtub with the aid of a ski pole I could no longer use for its rightful purpose.

The spring in Norman Wells was hot and dry. By the beginning of June, there were concerns about forest fires. On Monday June 5, Tim flew from Edmonton to Yellowknife and then onto Deline, a community on Great Bear Lake. He had been hired to complete a school inspection for the Board of Education. He would be there until Thursday and then fly on to Norman Wells for the night, and then fly back to Edmonton on the regular Friday afternoon flight.

A lightning strike at Fort Norman (now called Tuilta) on Tuesday June 6, began a fire that spread quickly. (Fort Norman was at the junction of the MacKenzie River and the Deline River.) An evacuation order was issued and the entire town was flown out to Norman Wells, 6 people at a time. Everyone was told to bring only a day pack. All animals were tied up and one person was left behind to feed them. If the fire got too close, he was ordered to untie them. It was thought that all the animals would make their way to the water instinctively and wait for the fire to pass. There was a boat that the man could use, should it be needed.

People in Norman Wells rallied around and everyone donated what they could. The school gym became a dorm for people who had no where else to go. The winds picked up on Wednesday and the fire crossed the Deline River and started making its way towards Norman Wells. Tim managed to fly into Norman Wells on Thursday evening and he said he had never seen anything like the fire making its way up the MacKenzie Valley.

1995: The fire moving up the Mackenzie River Photo courtesy JT Goddard

The fire siren went off about 8pm. We had been told to check the local TV station when the siren went off. Sure enough, the message came on, "Women and children make your way to the airport for immediate evacuation to Yellowknife."

The same rules applied to those leaving Fort Norman a few days previously: no pets and only day packs. We weren't part of that group—our children were in Edmonton with friends. We packed up the apartment, putting anything of value in the bathtub, only because bathtubs always seem to survive. The siren went off 3 or 4 times before midnight.

Each time we turned on the TV and the message was still the same. We could hear planes landing and taking off. We knew that there were a lot of women and children to take because of the evacuation of Fort Norman. Eventually, we went to bed. I had put foil over the windows in the bedroom so it was dark, even though it was daylight outside.

We woke up just before 6 am and turned on the radio. The CBC news came on and the broadcaster said, "The entire town of Norman Wells has been evacuated except for essential personnel. All non-essential people are in Yellowknife at the army base."

Tim and I looked at each other and then looked outside. There were no cars on the road, there were no people walking around, and there were no dogs barking. I had a cast on my leg that went from my knee to my foot. I didn't think I'd be any help fighting a fire. Tim volunteered to go and find someone. He wandered around and eventually found the emergency headquarters. He went inside and a woman came out, and asked, "Who are you?"

Tim explained that he was visiting me and the woman asked who I was. Once he explained about my broken leg, she said that I should have been on the first plane. Tim said that our children weren't with us, so we felt we should wait. This lead to a long discussion about where commas should go in disaster messages.

The upshot was that the woman gave a ticket to Tim for me for the afternoon flight. Tim already had a ticket. We made our way to the education office after breakfast only to find the director still there. He refused to leave his dog behind. His wife had gone but he stayed. The radio was on, full of news of the fire. I thought I'd better phone the girls and let them know where we were.

Nichola answered the phone. I explained that we were trying to leave Norman Wells because of the fire. To her everlasting shame she said, "Oh, okay. Can I wear your shoes to the dance tonight? Where are they?" I gave up trying to explain our life and death situation, told her where the shoes were, and said we might see her tonight. "Uh, okay," she responded.

Meanwhile, the radio kept saying that only essential personnel were left in Norman Wells. We got to the airport and checked in. The ticketing agent explained that all security personnel had been evacuated and we would be flying in an unsecured aircraft and would have to go through security when we got to Yellowknife.

We sat in the waiting room and waited. We heard some squeaking wheels and everyone turned and watched the cleaning lady wash the windows in the waiting area. The definition of essential and non essential blurred.

We flew to Yellowknife, cleared security, and then caught a flight to Edmonton and we were home in time to see Nichola before she went to the dance. The fire was stopped before it got to Norman Wells. I was out for about 10 days and then returned. In case you're interested, the dogs were cut loose in Fort Norman when the fire got very close to the houses. They all went to the water and all survived. When the people returned, they were reunited with their animals. There was even an extra dog that showed up that a family adopted.

When Tim began his studies in Edmonton, I promised him two years of study, after that he would have to go back to work. Almost two years to the day, he accepted a position as assistant professor of education at St. Francis Xavier University in Antigonish, Nova Scotia.

15. Antigonish, Nova Scotia September 1995 – June 1999

Tim's tenure-track contract at St. Francis Xavier University gave him an annual salary of $45,000. He could earn extra money teaching more courses, which he did. StFX had invited Tim out for an interview and offered him the job while he was there. He had time to find us a house before he returned to Edmonton. He found that we could not afford to rent a house in Antigonish.

People rented their houses out by the bedroom in town. It was usually between $450 and $550 a bedroom. We needed at least a three-bedroom house and on Tim's salary alone we couldn't afford the rent of $1350/month. Tim looked further out of town and found a three bedroom furnished house, high on the hill overlooking Ballantyne's Cove. The rent was $350/month and we could store all our things in the basement of the house. It was about a 40 minute drive into the university. It had a wonderful deck overlooking the wharf.

*1995 Winter Ballantyne's Cove house l-r: Victoria,
Nichola, Kate*

I applied for my Nova Scotia teaching certification but it was not a quick process. It was close to 6 months before I had a license. Meanwhile, the Nova Scotia Department of Education needed an education writer for correspondence courses. I began my work with them in the fall of 1995. The work continued until we left Nova Scotia.

Nichola started Grade 10 at Dr. John Hugh Gillis Memorial High School. Victoria was in her last year of junior high, and Kate was enrolled in Grade 1 at the RH MacDonald Elementary School in Maryvale.

Although the view from the house was lovely, it was a three-season house. Heating the house in the winter cost more monthly than the rent. We started looking for houses and eventually found one on the Old Maryvale

Road, closer to town, but the girls could continue at the same school.

1997 House on the Old Maryvale Road

We then could finally get a dog. Actually, it ended up being two dogs who had the run of 50 acres around our house. One was a black lab called Oggy, and the other was Cropper, a mutt from the SPCA that looked like a half-sized Irish wolfhound. I think the English refer to them as lurchers. We would let them out in the morning and they would disappear into the bush. They would return when they were called.

Late one afternoon the dogs returned to the house. Cropper could hardly breathe. He obviously had something stuck in his throat. Tim arrived just after the dogs and I said to him, "I'll phone the vet. You'll probably have to take him into town."

I called the vet's office and because it was after 6pm there was going to be a $75 callout fee plus the cost of retrieving whatever it was that was stuck. We had people coming for dinner. I kept cooking and Tim took the cheque book and Cropper and started back to town. The wheezing got worse and Tim started driving faster.

Just before the vet clinic, there was a small bridge that

was slightly humped. The car went up in the air and returned to the ground with a thump. The thump was enough to make Cropper throw up the bone. Tim turned into the road leading to the vet's office. The vet was waiting for the emergency. The dog was sitting on the front seat, wagging his tail. Tim got out of the car, wrote a cheque for $75, explaining to the vet what had happened, and then drove home.

I had applied for a job at StFx as the International Student Coordinator. The office called on the Friday and asked if I could come in for an interview on Labour Day. The phone rang early on Sunday morning. It was the son of a physics professor from the University of Papua New Guinea who had our names and phone number from a professor of Education at UPNG who had done his PhD with Tim at the University of Alberta.

Ahmed explained that it had taken him a week to get from Vancouver to Antigonish. Air Canada had gone on strike and he took whatever flights going east he could get. He had no idea where his luggage was and he had to register at the university today. He asked for help. He had spent the night at a B&B which was close to us. I picked him up and took him to the university and joined the lineup of other parents dropping off their children. Ironically, that same day, many miles away, Nichola was joining the 1st year class at the Royal Military College in Kingston, Ontario.

I soon realized that Ahmed, who was originally from

Sierra Leone, needed a lot of help. I contacted friends who had 5 sons and they gave him some clothes. He could not access any money until the bank opened on Tuesday. Tim and I gave him a loan so that he could buy the 'Freshman Pack' which included a pillowcase stuffed with junk food and StFX swag. He also needed sheets, towels, and blankets. Tim brought those to him from our house. By lunchtime, he was as settled as he could be.

When I went to my interview the next day, and they asked me what skills I would bring to the job, I was able to give them a first-hand account of what was needed. I was given the job and a shared office that I could only use in the afternoon. It was 2 hours a day and the students dropped by with problems and ideas. It was the beginning of universities trying to attract foreign students as a way of increasing revenue. What began in 1998 with 12 students has blossomed across Canada.

Just after New Year's Day, Ahmed arrived at my office. Ahmed's mother had called and told him that his father had gone back to Sierra Leone for Christmas, leaving his wife and son in Papua New Guinea. He hadn't been heard from since. I told him I wasn't sure that I could help. After he left, I turned on the computer and began searching for the Canadian Embassy in Sierra Leone. The internet was in its infancy in 1998 and all I could find was an email address for the Canadian Embassy in Niger. I sent an email explaining the situation and asking if they could help in any way.

When I arrived at work the next day, the office was all abuzz. Ottawa had called looking for me. I called the number they had left.

The man who answered immediately, said "Is your student's father on a Canadian passport?"

I replied that he wasn't.

He said, "Civil war has broken out in Freetown, the capital. If the man is on one side of the river, he's probably okay. If he's on the other side, he's probably dead. There's not much we can do but give your student this number and he can call whenever he likes for updates."

I thanked him and hung up, amazed by the speed that information was able to travel from Niger to Ottawa and then Antigonish. I phoned Ahmed and relayed what I had learned and gave him the phone number.

The next day I got to work and the same man had left a message asking me to call him back immediately. I did. He said, "We have a helicopter going into Freetown later today to pick up Canadians. They are willing to take a message to your student's father if you can get an address."

I thanked them again, and immediately called Ahmed. There was no answer. It was lunchtime on a university campus. I called security and soon had men scouring the campus, looking for him. They eventually found him and he arrived at my office. I shared my news. He said, "Don't worry. My dad phoned this morning. He's out of the country and on his way back to Port Moresby. He's fine."

I breathed a sigh of relief and called my person in Ottawa. His answering machine kicked in and I left a message, explaining that Ahmed had heard from his father. He was safe and out of the country. I thanked them for their help and hung up. After work, I drove the

20 minutes to our house. There was a message from Ottawa on our home phone. "Can you ask Ahmed how his father got out? We have Canadians who are trapped there and we are trying to find ways to evacuate them."

I called Ahmed and asked him. He said his father hadn't told him but once he found out he would let me know. I called Ottawa and let them know. Several weeks later, he found out that his father escaped with some Arabs in a private plane. By then it was too late.

Tim found himself teaching graduate courses all over Nova Scotia, usually on the weekends because that was when teachers were available. He returned on Saturday evenings and often spent Sundays in the office, catching up. When the University of Calgary advertised a position in his field, working with PhD students, he applied. StFx did not have a PhD program.

As we got ready to move from Antigonish to Calgary, we decided that the dogs would fly rather than drive. We sold the house much faster than we expected. This meant that we had to get the dogs to the kennels just outside of Halifax before the movers arrived. It just so happened that a visiting scholar from England had to be picked up at the Halifax airport on the same day. As far as I was concerned it was a win-win situation. I would drop off the dogs, have lunch with a friend in Halifax, and then pick the academic up when the flight from London got in around 2:30. Not only that, the university would pay me mileage.

I got the dogs in the car and had invested in a box of dog treats thinking that they might be a little unsure of the kennels but they were both extremely food motivated and would go anywhere if food was offered. I was just about to leave when the phone rang. I thought it might be the packers as they were due in that day so I answered the call. By the time I finished, and got back in the car, the box of dog treats had been demolished.

I started on my journey. Cropper was in the front seat, and Oggy, the black lab was sprawled on the back seat. Everything was fine until we got on the 4 lane highway in Truro. Cropper started circling on the front seat, and then without warning, had the most incredible projectile diarrhea against the dashboard of the car. He then jumped in the back seat, and repeated the procedure. Oggy moved enough so she wasn't covered.

I was doing 110 km/hr and thought about stopping but then realized that there was nothing I could do. I had nothing to clean up the mess and hopefully, Cropper had gotten rid of whatever it was that had caused his upset, probably the dog treats.

As I drove along, I suddenly remembered that I had to pick up the visiting scholar. At that point, I wasn't sure what I was going to do. I arrived at the kennels. The woman came out and came to the car. The dogs shot out of the car like bullets and ran straight into the kennels. The woman produced a small bowl with some disinfectant in the water and gave me a rag. I did what I could but I needed something with industrial strength.

I left the dogs and drove the half hour into Halifax. It was a hot July day and I opened all the windows because you couldn't breathe if the windows were shut. My friend worked for the provincial Department of Education and I parked in the multi-story car park next to the building where she worked. As I drove in, I saw a sign saying, "Danger! High theft area. Please lock your car." Now, I thought, there's a solution. If someone stole the car, I could rent one. It would be clean and odour free. I left the windows open and didn't lock the doors. I stopped short of leaving the keys in the ignition.

When I got back after lunch, the car was still there. I had to go to Plan B. I knew there was a car wash out at the airport and I thought if I picked up some doggy-doo shampoo and some paper towels and slipped the guy an extra $20 he might spray the inside of the car. I picked up the supplies and drove to the airport and found the car wash. I got out of the car and the attendant came over and said, "Can I help you, Miss?'

I explained my day as quickly as I could. He was certainly appreciative of my story. When I finally finished, he looked and me and said, "I'd love to help you but we've had a freak electrical storm and we have no power or water."

I got back in the car. I really hadn't thought of a Plan C. I had an hour until the plane arrived. There was another gas station at the next exit. I didn't know if it had a car wash but it was worth a try. There was no car wash, so I parked in the parking lot and I opened all 4 doors and did what I could with the doggy-doo shampoo and the paper towels. In my enthusiasm or perhaps my despera-tion, I completely soaked the front passenger seat. Not to be deterred, I went to the Dollar Store and bought matching fluffy beach towels and arranged them on the two front seats. Then I drove to the airport. Once we'd met, my first question to him, "Do you like dogs?"

Luckily he said he loved them and we spent the trip home talking about dogs. This happened more than 20 years ago. We still see the visiting scholar from time to time and he always tells me that he couldn't smell anything.

16. Calgary, Alberta July 1999 – August 2008

W e were fortunate to find a house for rent that allowed us to have dogs, and quickly settled into life in the big city. We lived in the northwest and were able to go for long walks on Nose Hill, one of the largest urban parks in Canada.

Initially, I was given a one year contract as Literacy Coordinator in the Faculty of Education at the University of Calgary. It was a spousal hire and awkward on many levels. I did not renew the contract and began substitute teaching with the Calgary Board of Education. I wrote a book called 'Subbing in the City' telling 26 different stories about my time as a substitute teacher, one story for each letter of the alphabet. This is the entry for B.

On one memorable September I was called to a junior high school to sub for a Humanities teacher who was going home because of illness. She stayed at the school until I arrived to tell me what to do with her students. There were notes on the board for the Social Studies and Language Arts classes and then she started talking about her band classes. "The Grade 7s just got their instruments yesterday so let them make noise. They are really excited about their instruments. The Handbell class has older students and they'll know what to do. Please make sure they wear gloves."

In due course the Grade 7s arrived in the music room. I introduced myself and asked them to get their instruments out and see if they could make a noise with them. Out came the flutes, the French horns, the trombones, the tubas, trumpets, and clarinets. One student found the paddles for the bass drum. There were about 5 students without instruments because they'd forgotten them at home or were away when they were distributed. So these students drifted over to the piano and started pounding on the keys.

At this point the vice principal wandered in to see if everything was alright. I said that it was but I felt a period was too long for the students just to 'make noise.' The piano was particularly piercing. She looked at me and asked what the students were supposed to be doing.

"Trying to make noise," I told her.

She asked, "Can you stand it for the rest of the period if I take the piano players?"

I readily agreed. Once the piano players left, the room seemed remarkably quiet.

The next period was Handbells for a group of Grade 7- 9 students. Before they arrived, I looked in the cupboard for handbells but couldn't find any. I asked the students when they arrived if they knew where the handbells were kept but no one knew. So I picked up the phone and asked the school secretary where the handbells were. She responded, "They are supposed to be there. Are you sure?"

I told her that neither myself nor the students could find them . She somewhat grudgingly agreed to look for them. Luckily the students were pleasant and understanding. After about 10 minutes, there was a knock at the door and two students were there with suitcases containing the handbells.

The students got up to get the bells. "Make sure you put the gloves on before you touch the bells," I reminded them.

"Where are the gloves?" asked one of the students.

I picked up the phone. Again, the secretary answered. I thanked her for finding the bells and wondered if she knew where the gloves were. She responded, "Are you sure?"

I assured her they were not there. She said that she would see what she could find out.

After a few minutes, there was another knock at the door and a student came in with a grocery store bag filled with white gloves. Again the students rose, put on the gloves, retrieved the bells, and sat back in their seats. I said, "Go ahead and play. Your teacher said you would know what to do."

"Where's the music?" asked one of the students.

"I have absolutely no idea," I replied. I didn't have enough nerve to call the office again, so I had the students return the bells to the suitcases, take off the gloves and return them to the grocery store bag. They then returned to their seats and it was decided that we would talk about any topic that came to mind. When the vice principal came to the classroom this time, she asked why the students were talking and not playing handbells. I explained what had happened. She left me to it.

After a year of subbing, I accepted a one year contract, teaching Humanities to junior high school students. I taught two Grade 8 English classes and one Grade 7. The school hosted a 'Meet the Teacher' night in the third week of school. Parents arrived expecting me to know how their child was doing. I had marked a couple of small assignments, but nothing that would pass or fail a student. One mother stood in line, desperate to talk about her son. When she finally sat in front of me she explained that Bill had failed Grade 7 Humanities and she was extremely worried about him in Grade 8 at a new school. There were three Bills in this class. I had no idea which one he was. I said it was early days and I hadn't seen too many problems. I told her I would contact her if anything went wrong.

Bill, actually all three of them, did just fine in my English class. The Bill who had failed Grade 7 did his homework and assignments and wrote tests. He wasn't setting the world on fire but he was okay.

That Grade 8 class was selected to attend school at Calgary Olympic Park for a week. The classroom was on top of the ski jump. The introductory talk was done by one of the organizers, who mentioned that if a student did a certain number of volunteer hours, they could earn a free ski pass.

There was an interview that was part of the volunteer process. Bill talked to me about becoming a volunteer. I asked the organizers if they could add a mock interview during the week. They did, and after Bill applied, had an interview, and was accepted. Eventually, he got a free ski pass.

By the end of the year, I put Bill's name forward as the most improved English student. He'd gone from failing to passing. On the way, he'd volunteered. He was given the award. I had the pleasure of phoning his mother to tell her. She burst into tears. Bill arrived for prize day wearing a new suit.

When the year ended, I had to return to the sub pool. Luckily, I was asked to work on a project with the North Battleford Friendship Centre, introducing residential schools to elementary students. I made a number of trips to North Battleford but the last one was the most memorable.

My friend, Arlene, and I were driving from Calgary, Alberta to North Battleford, Saskatchewan in early June. On the way, we left the highway at Hobbema because I wanted to find the place name of one of the buildings for a story I was writing. We found it and as we turned to leave the reserve, we saw a sandwich board sign that read "Neckbone dinner - $5.00/plate." The dinner didn't open for a couple of hours so we didn't stop. As we drove the rest of the way, we chatted about what kind of neckbones were used—turkey or chicken or beef—and wondered what vegetables would be served alongside.

We overnighted and then made our way to the print shop we were using and had a meeting with the people making our booklets. Then we got to the Friendship Centre and found that we were no longer employed. There had been an election and the new council had different prioities. We went for lunch and talked about what we should do. Arlene said, "I think we should treat today like a holiday. I picked up a brochure at the print shop today that talks about an English knot garden and tea room near Kindersley. It's about 2 ½ hours from here." She then went on to explain that it closed at 5pm so if we were going to go, we have to leave now as it was close to 2pm.

We figured we could get something to eat at the tea room and then drive the 4 hours back to Calgary. We hopped in the car and drove due south. When we arrived in Kindersley, Arlene gave me the directions and we got on a smaller paved road, a dirt road, and finally, we arrived at a trailer whose sign indicated the English Knot Garden was around the back. Sure enough, there was a knot garden, and on the other side, was the tea room. We followed the path and were met at the door by a woman who was wearing a dress that reminded me of the wardrobes of women in movies like *Pride and Prejudice*.

She welcomed us warmly and invited us in. "Have you ever been here before?" she asked. We shook our heads so she continued. "This is our gift shop," and she waved her arms, "And through that door, you are in the tea room. Would you like tea?"

Arlene and I both said yes and the woman led us to the tea room. As we entered you couldn't help but notice the dozen or so white plastic rectangular tables covered with clear plastic tablecloths and surrounded by white plastic chairs. She then began to give us instructions. She pointed to a wall of china tea cups. "Take the one you'd like to drink from and choose a table and I'll bring over a menu." We did as we were told and the woman brought the menus. She suggested we pick our tea from the 150 choices. We decided that we would just have black tea, just normal black tea. The woman went off to get the tea.

Arlene said, "We're the only customers. Do you think we're the first people she's had today?"

The woman returned carrying a tray with a teapot with a sponge attached to the spout of the teapot by an elastic band that went over the knob of the lid. She had 2 teabags, each on separate saucers. The teapot was filled with hot water and the sponge was to catch any drips. She then asked us if we'd like anything to eat and we decided on the Devonshire Cream Tea. The woman went bustling back to the kitchen. We put the tea bags in the teapot and waited for the tea to steep. Meanwhile, we could hear whirring sounds coming from the kitchen. Then the noise stopped and the woman reappeared with her hands behind her back. We looked at her.

She said, "You girls look like you would enjoy licking these!" and she produced the two beaters covered in whipped cream from behind her back. She proceeded to give us each one and then she left. Arlene and I looked at each other, not quite sure what to do. I said, "Do we look that hungry?" and Arlene replied, "How many other people do you think have licked these?" Luckily, we found some tissue in our pockets and were able to wipe the cream off so it looked like we had licked them.

The Devonshire Cream Tea was not for purists, as

whipped cream was used instead of English clotted cream but it tasted fine to us and we enjoyed the atmosphere and the bizarre gift of the beaters. As we were leaving, the woman said to us, "All of us tour operators encourage people to try other places and I think you would enjoy the Great Wall of Saskatchewan." It was only 8km away and we thought it might be fun. We got the instructions and proceeded to the spot. (If you are interested it is 1.6 km west of Smiley, Saskatchewan on Highway 772.) There was a tour bus leaving as we arrived. We read on the sign that Albert Johnston, the farmer who owned the land, from 1962—1991 cleared stones off his farmland and used them to build a self-supporting wall. The end result was a little over ½ km in length. Arlene and I drove around the wall and as we left, wondered how many people actually come to this spot annually.

About a year after this, I was working on a reserve, and invited to have neckbone dinner. Finally, I thought, the mystery would be solved. It was pork neckbones, available at many supermarkets. They could be boiled, fried, or baked, and served with anything. It took me a year, but I'd solved the mystery.

I thought that I might have to go back to subbing, but then Onion Lake, a Cree reserve near Lloydminster, called and asked if I could help in the establishment of a Cree language immersion program. I accepted and drove up to see where I would be living. As I unpacked I found a hunting rifle in the bedroom cupboard. I left it there.

The next day when I went to the office and told my new boss there was a gun in my closet. "We told you it came fully furnished," he said, laughing.

For the first couple of months, I would drive 6 hours on Sunday to get to my apartment and then drive 6 hours back on Friday afternoons to get home. It was not sustainable, and I eventually drove up one week a month and worked from home the rest of the time. When the driving got too much, I began flying and rented a car at the Lloydminster airport. This went on until we left Calgary.

Meanwhile, Nichola graduated from the Royal Military College in the spring of 2002 and was posted to the 1st Regiment, Royal Canadian horse Artillery. This was her dream assignment and she moved to the base in Shilo, near Brandon, Manitoba. She married Jason Beam that December.

2002 RMC Nichola's graduation l-r: Tim, Kate, Nichola, Victoria, Sally

2002 Nichola and her grandfather at the RMC ball
after graduation

Victoria completed Grade 12 in Calgary and enrolled in the Bachelor of Humanities program at Carleton University in Ottawa. Kate opted for the French Immersion program when she completed Grade 6 and joined the debating team as well as the Army cadets. We were settled into life in Calgary

There was a constant procession of friends and relatives, including Tim's mother, who visited from Wales a couple of times a year. She learned the transit system and made a group of friends that took her to a variety of places. Life in Llangwnnadl was pretty quiet and she enjoyed the hustle and bustle of Calgary.

Bill and Pat arrived for a week's holiday with us when we lived in Calgary. They were friends of Tim's parents and Bill had given Tim his first job delivering papers

and helped him return from Belgium when he had lost his passport. Tim was glad to have them come and stay but was only going to be with them for one night as he had to leave the day after their arrival for a project in Kosovo.

We gave them our bedroom as our guest room had bunk beds and we couldn't see them climbing up and down the ladder. He was in his mid 70s and liked good food and wine. In any case, Tim was leaving and I could sleep in one of the beds in the guest room. I cleaned out our room and they took it over.

Tim left on an early morning flight and by the time I got back to the house, Kate was helping them with breakfast and Victoria was getting ready for work. The phone rang just as I got in and friends of ours invited us to a BBQ. I explained that Tim's parents friends' were with us. "No problem," they said. "Bring them along."

I told them we'd been invited out for a BBQ and Pat immediately said, "I have to wash my hair."

I said, "There are two bathrooms. Just pick the one you'd like to use."

To which Pat replied, "You don't understand. I've never washed my own hair. I need a hairdresser."

So, I eventually found a hairdresser and Pat got her hair done.

They were ready for the BBQ. Bill had on a 3 piece suit and Pat wore a blue chiffon dress. They asked me if I was getting changed as I was wearing the clothes I'd worn all day. I replied, "It's a BBQ. I think I'll go as I am."

I drove them to our friends' house and we all got out of the car. I rang the doorbell and there was no answer.

"No, worries, " I said. "They must be round the back. I'll just go and see."

I went round the back and there was no one there. As I returned to the front of the house, I realized that I had obviously not heard the day when we were invited. I'd have to phone and ask them what day they meant. Meanwhile, we went home, stopping for fish and chips on the way.

When I phoned our friends, they explained it was the next night. And Bill and Pat wore their party clothes again the next night. The only good thing was that Pat didn't have to get her hair done again.

I think they had a good time and when the end of the week came, I was almost sorry to see them go, but excited to get back into my bed. They were travelling to Lake Louise and were going to spend a night at Chateau Lake Louise. I wasn't clear of their itinerary after that but knew they were planning on flying to England from Vancouver in about two weeks.

As we said our goodbyes, Bill said, "If we've left anything behind, just keep it. I hate it when people expect you to send them things they've left."

So off they went, and I made a beeline for the bedroom. I started taking the sheets off the bed and noticed a pile of paper on one side of the bed. I moved the top paper and found all their English credit cards and about £400 in cash. I did the only thing I could do. Victoria and I drove to Chateau Lake Louise and left an envelope with the cash and credit cards. It took over five hours but I didn't really think he meant me to keep them. They did call and thank me.

As my parents got older, my sisters and I took it in turns to visit them in the Soo. On one trip, I found myself sitting at a gate in the Toronto International Airport waiting for a flight to Calgary, minding my own business. A woman walked past with her husband. She saw that there were a couple of seats beside me and she stopped and turned to her husband, and commanded him to sit down. He tried to say something but she turned to him and said quite vehemently, "For God's sake, just sit down and shut up."

She arranged herself in the seat next to mine and her husband sat down beside her. She turned to me and said, "Do you know what he did?"

I certainly had no idea but was dying to find out.

She carried on. I don't think it would have mattered if I had said I wasn't interested. She would have told me anyway. "Well", she continued, "We live in St John's and our daughter lives near Vancouver. We decided that we would go and visit and thought it would be good idea to go in January. The fares are cheaper and the weather home is terrible."

At that point she drew breath and her husband said, "We have…" but she turned to him and said, "Shut up, you've already made such a mess of things." He sat quietly, almost like the family dog.

She picked up the story where she had left off. " My husband is retired and I told him to book the tickets for us. He did. The day before we were to leave, we took the dog to the kennels. The next morning, there had been a huge dump of snow overnight and the taxi couldn't make it down our street on account that the roads hadn't been plowed. We got our suitcases and pulled them through the snow up to the main road. A taxi met us there and took us to the airport. We stood in line for ages, waiting to check in. When we finally got to the front of the queue, the Air Canada agent told us our tickets were for the next day. I was that mad I couldn't speak. We took our bags, found a taxi who dropped us off at the top of our street and we pulled our suitcases through the snow to our house. The only good thing was that the snow was cleared during the night and the taxi could get to our house the next day. And so here we are."

The husband made one final attempt to say something to his wife. She acknowledged him and said, "Well, what's so important now?"

And he said, "They've been calling our names. I think we've missed our flight to Vancouver."

She stood up, brushed off her skirt, and said, "Why didn't you tell me?"

He smiled weakly at me, and off they went in search of their flight to Vancouver.

We spent Christmas 2005 in Wales with Tim's family. Nichola and her husband came from Shilo, Victoria flew from Toronto where she was in the PhD Medieval Studies program, Kate and I came from Calgary, and Tim arrived from Kosovo. Unlike other Christmases there was an air of uneasiness. We knew Nichola was going to

Afghanistan in the new year. It wasn't until she spread the map of Afghanistan and Pakistan out on her grand-mother's dining room table, the reality began to sink in. I thought, initially, that she would wear a blue beret and help to keep the peace. It wasn't until she said, "We are making the peace, not keeping it," that all of us realized that she was undertaking a job that was far more complex and dangerous that we first thought.

By the end of January, Nichola was in Afghanistan, and we put phones in every room so we wouldn't miss her calls. We knew that she was not often at the base in Kandahar, that she was happier outside the wire. On May 17th, 2006, her father's birthday, she was killed. Much has been written about her life and legacy. We have learned to live with this tragedy but it hasn't been easy. We have to be careful not to say, 'if only' because that doesn't change anything. Victoria told me once that we have to remember her, not wallow in her memory. Some days are better than others.

After Nichola's death, we muddled along. We both went back to work, Tim at the University of Calgary and I continued with the Cree Immersion program. Victoria and Kate kept us grounded in reality. We made it through the first year and hosted a sagali—a feast for the dead in Trobriand Island culture—and invited everyone who had helped us through that first year. I took 4 months leave from my job and managed to complete my MA with thesis and graduated in May 2008.

Wherever we went there were memories of being there with Nichola. We were often recognized as being the parents of the soldier that was killed. When Tim was offered a position as Dean of Education at the University of Prince Edward Island, we jumped at the opportunity. We had never lived there so there would be no ghosts to confront us.

When Tim left the University of Calgary he was over 55, so therefore, according to the HR department, he was retiring and was given the title Professor Emeritus. The Faculty Association contacted me to ask what he would like as a retirement gift. I was facing the prospect of packing the house and didn't think we needed any more things. I suggested they make a donation to a charity we were working with at that point in time.

I told Tim what I had done when he returned home from work, and he said, "I have no idea how much money they spend on these gifts. If anyone else asks you, tell them he wants Scotch."

The next day I was at the university and the woman organizing Tim's retirement gift saw me and said she had been unable to get through to the charity. I responded immediately. "Don't worry about the donation. He wants Scotch."

At the retirement party, Tim was given a gift certificate for $450 to a liquor store in Calgary that had one of the best Scotch selections. A few weeks later, I dropped Tim and a friend off at the store. Two hours later I returned. The two men got into the car and one of the staff placed a carton in the back. All I could smell was Scotch.

From what I have been able to piece together, they started off tasting the Scotch that was $400/bottle but realized that it was only one bottle. Eventually, having tasted many, they picked 7 different bottles, paid for them, and the clerk placed them in a cardboard carton. Tim said that it seemed wrong to have an odd number in the box, so he paid for another so now there were 8 bottles.

Over the next month or so different people stopped by the house and added to Tim's collection. Ultimately, there were 12 bottles of fine Scotch. Tim was concerned about where the Scotch would be in the car as he was flying out to Charlottetown and Victoria and I were driving. Eventually, it was decided that the best place would be on the floor right behind the driver's seat, surrounded by pillows and blankets. If we were front-ended or rear-ended the Scotch would be safe.

Just before we were about to leave, another bottle of Scotch appeared. There was no room in the carton and at that point in time, we were placing bottles of wine and liquors that had not been opened in the wheel well, well wrapped in bubble wrap. I thought the last bottle of Scotch might as well go there.

It took us 8 days, stopping along the way to visit family and friends. When we finally arrived in Charlotte-town, the moving truck had just finished taking our goods and chattels into the house. Although Tim was happy to see us, he was more interested in how his Scotch had travelled. It arrived safely and was carefully stored and doled out over the next few years.

17. 45 PARKSIDE DRIVE, CHARLOTTETOWN, PRINCE EDWARD ISLAND

Just after we moved in, I got a job with the Department of Education as an itinerant EAL—English as an Additional Language (ESL)—teacher. I was assigned several non-English speaking students at the two high schools where I provided classroom support as well as tutoring when necessary. In December as I was leaving one of the schools I missed a step and fell down a flight of stairs, breaking several ribs. As I found out, there was not much that could be done for broken ribs except rest, giving them a chance to heal.

While I was recuperating I got a call from one of my sisters to tell me that my mother had died. My parents lived in the same house in Sault Ste Marie for over 50 years. They eventually had a chairlift put in to make the upstairs accessible. My mother said the only way she was leaving the house was feet first. That happened just after we moved to Prince Edward Island.

In December 2008, the mother-in-law of one of my sisters died. My sister returned to the Soo for the funeral and then spent the weekend visiting with my parents. She left on the Monday, and another sister's husband arrived to stay with my parents as his father was quite ill. He was in the living room working one morning when he heard the chairlift come down. He said good morning to my father who proceeded into the kitchen and made tea for my mother. My father took the chairlift back up with tea for my mother. A short time later, it came back down.

My father walked into the living room, carrying the teacup, and said to my brother-in-law, "I think Kathleen's dead. Can you come with me and check?" As my father was a doctor and had been a coroner for a number of years, my father probably knew but my brother-in-law went anyway. There was no doubt about it. She had died in her sleep, just the way she had wanted. They arrived back in the kitchen and my father said, "Let's have a cup of tea and figure out what we are going to do." That's what they did.

We were all called in due course and made our way to the Soo. I arrived first, without luggage, and my father said, "I think you should have your mother's room. Look in her chest of drawers for a nightie. Don't worry, the sheets have been changed."

"Thanks," I said.

I went up to my mother's room and opened the door. It still smelled like her. I don't think I had ever opened my mother's drawers so I was a little hesitant. I opened the top one. There was a carton of cigarettes, opened. My mother had said that she had quit smoking a number of years ago but obviously, had kept a stash. Occasionally when I visited I thought I could smell cigarette smoke, but never dreamed that it was my mother. No wonder she needed the fan. I opened the second drawer. There was an opened bottle of gin. I can see her even now, fan blowing, having an illicit cigarette and swigging gin from the bottle. She died at 83. I am glad she had those indulgences.

I got into her bed and discovered that the mattress seemed more like a thermarest. I don't think that it had ever been replaced. When my mother complained about it, my father found a piece of plywood to go in between the mattress and the springs. There were never any complaints after that. I was so tired I fell asleep without moving much.

The next day my husband arrived and joined me in my mother's bed. We got as comfortable as we could and Tim said to me, "Do you hear that?"

We listened and there were scratching noises in the bedroom ceiling that got louder and louder and then stopped, only to start up again a few minutes later. After a restless night, we called the exterminators in the morning. The attic had become a winter den for several squirrels and they had made a hole so they could get in and out easily. It was a party place. My mother always denied being deaf but she must have been deaf as a post not to have heard those acrobatic squirrels. The exterminator arrived the next day and plugged a large hole in the eaves that the squirrels had used for years, the guy told us, as their own doorway into their apartment.

We bought a house in Charlottetown, close enough to the university should Tim want to walk. The possession date was June 1st. I flew out the day before and did the inspection with the real estate agent. I had bought three hockey bags full of towels and linens. We were getting new beds delivered the next day so I would be able to sleep in the house. A friend arrived from Halifax to help. We had a busy week. I dropped her off at the bus on Friday and then went back to the house to pack before leaving from the airport. The previous owners had left an Island Waste Management Collection calendar but it was like reading Greek to me. I ended up putting the garbage in hockey bags and taking it back to Calgary. Tim picked me up at the airport and asked me if I had any luggage. I sheepishly told him about the garbage.

Tim flew to Charlottetown about three weeks later. He phoned me the first night and said he couldn't understand my confusion. "It was all in the sorting," he said, "I have hung plastic bags from the kitchen cupboards. There's one for compost, one for recycle, one for plastics, and one for waste." I remarked that he had figured it out better than me.

At the end of the week, I met his plane. I asked him if he had any luggage. "Just the garbage," he said. "The garbage was sorted but I couldn't put it in the bins because no one would at the house for six weeks. Then I didn't know where compost went and I wasn't sure about plastic. I ran out of time and brought everything back with me." I smiled.

The new house had a working hot tub on the back deck. We'd never owned one and in the beginning it was pretty exciting. Tim agreed to look after the chemical balance which had to be tested and adjusted on a regular basis. There was one noticeable slip-up when a friend of ours who arrived from Calgary got into the hot tub and her bathing suit changed colour. We took possession of the house June 1st and kept the hot tub going throughout the winter so when the girls came home they could use it.

In the spring a family stayed with us and enjoyed splashing around. When they left, the water in the hot tub was stone cold. I called the local hot tub store and the woman said to me, "Can you get to the hot tub with your phone?" I said I could and she said that she wanted me to open the control panel She explained where it was and then told me to punch in a series of numbers and then hit the okay tab. She felt that the kids might have inadvertently changed the setting. Putting the numbers in would reboot the system. She said, "Give it 24 hours and it should be fixed."

Twenty-four hour later, I checked the water. It was still stone cold. I called the hot tub people. The same woman answered the phone and said, "Can you get to the hot tub with your phone?" I said we had already done that. She said, "Humour me. Do it one more time." So I did. Twenty-four hours later I called her and explained that nothing had changed. She said, "I guess we had better get the technicians out. I can't tell you when they will show up." I said it really didn't matter as the hot tub was outside.

Two weeks later, Tim and I arrived home and found bits and pieces of hot tub scattered over the lawn. I called the hot tub store. I explained who I was and she immediately said, "You have bees. The guys can't do anything until you get rid of the bees." I asked her who I should call. You could almost hear the shrug of her shoulders through the phone line. "Try the yellow pages and look for exterminators." I called the first exterminator and explained the problem. He asked, "Are they bees or wasps?" I said I didn't know. He explained that if they were bees, he couldn't kill them and I'd have to get a farmer to catch them. If they were wasps, he'd be able to take care of them. He arrived, dressed in a white haz-mat suit. He saw immediately that they were wasps who had made nests in the insulating foam surrounding the hot tub. For $125 he sprayed everywhere and told us in 24 hours the technicians could come back as all the wasps would be dead.

The next day I called the woman at the hot tub store. She told me she would tell the guys. The men returned, put everything back together and told us we needed new filters. Once we put them in, the hot tub would be up and running. So for another $175 we bought new filters. We popped them in and waited the requisite 24 hours. The water was still stone cold. I called the store. The woman said to me, "Can you get to the hot tub with your phone?" We sold the hot tub shortly thereafter to an engineer who felt he could fix it.

There was a large hole left in the deck after the hot tube had gone. A friend offered to rebuild it. He got all the supplies he needed and asked me if he could get the jack from the Subaru. I gave him the keys and he came back with the jack as well as a few more things. We had all completely forgotten the Scotch and other alcoholic bottles put in the wheel well. For two years it had travelled with us and survived two Maritime winters. The Scotch was even better than it would have been had we consumed it 2 years earlier.

I decided that being an itinerant EAL was not what I wanted to do and found part time work at the Atlantic Veterinary College at the University of Prince Edward Island. Eventually, I was referred to as the Educational Specialist, and worked with faculty to enhance their teaching. It was a fabulous job which I kept until I retired in the spring of 2022. It was a flexible arrangement and allowed me time to do other things.

Victoria graduated with a PhD in Medieval Studies and after some travel and a few jobs to support herself, is now a fulltime fantasy novelist. She went to Boston in the fall of 2022 for a book launch and hosted a meeting of one of her fan clubs. She had another fan club meeting in Canberra for Australian fans when she traveled there in January 2023.

Kate graduated as a lawyer from McGill several years ago and is current working with start up companies in a large law office in Vancouver. She has a house on the Sunshine Coast and a dog called Sheamus.

2017 Kate's called to the Ontario bar l-r: Victoria and Kate

When my father was 90, he learned that his youngest brother in Halifax was not doing well and losing his faculties. He called me in Charlottetown and asked if I would take him from Sault Ste Marie to visit his brother as soon as we could go. He would pay. He wanted to see his brother while he could still talk to him, not at his funeral . When I checked for tickets online, the only ones I could find on the flight between Toronto and Halifax were middle seats and I thought how difficult it would be for him. I suggested that he buy business class seats. He agreed.

When we checked in at the Sault Ste Marie airport and I saw the 'Priority' stickers go on the suitcases, I realized that the trip was going to be very different from my flight from Charlottetown to Sault Ste Marie. My father and I would be the ones people looked at enviously as they walked through the front of the plane to the seats behind the curtain. It had been a while since my father had flown and he suffered the indignity of having his nail scissors confiscated.

"What would I do with scissors," he huffed. "I can't even get out of this seat."

There was no business class on the flight between the Soo and Toronto, but it was a whole new world on the flight between Toronto and Halifax. They called him Dr West and took his coat and hung it up for him. They brought him orange juice as we waited for take off. Then, they spread a white linen tablecloth on the tray in front of him. They showed him how to button the cloth napkin into his shirt and served him a hot meal and offered him a drink. As we got off the plane, my father remarked, "I don't understand why people hate flying."

I let it go.

Of course, our luggage was the first off the plane, thanks to the 'Priority' stickers. We picked up a very large car at the airport because my father wanted to be able to take my aunt and uncle out as neither of them were driving at this point. My father asked if I knew where they lived. I said that it really didn't matter because I had my GPS. My father asked, "Is it a map?". I said. "Not really. It tells me where to go."

When I first got my GPS, it was set to a female voice that my husband thought sounded like Margaret Thatcher so I changed it to the male voice. My father was transfixed by the voice of Richard and marvelled at the ability of the machine to get us from the airport to downtown Halifax.

It was dark by the time we arrived at my aunt and uncle's condo. It was not a great time for a visit so my aunt suggested that we go for a picnic the next day. I think my aunt had this romantic vision of what she and my uncle used to do when visitors came. She suggested I pick them up at 11 am. My father and I returned to the hotel with Richard's calm, unflappable voice guiding us there. As money appeared to be no object with my father, I arranged concierge parking so when we arrived at the hotel, I helped my father out of the car and gave the keys to the doorman.

The next morning I asked for the car for 10:45 and by the time we arrived in the lobby, the car was waiting for us. The doorman opened the door for my father and helped him settle. He then loaded my father's walker in the back of the car. As we were driving to the condo, my father said, "I'm glad the doorman helped me in. I slipped last week and went right under the car. Luckily, there was a football player close by and he managed to haul me out." He said it in such a matter-of-fact-way that I laughed. I brushed aside all the 'what could have happened' and enjoyed the moment.

We arrived at the condo at exactly 11 am. My aunt, true to her English roots, had filled a wicker picnic basket with china plates, sandwiches without crusts, cans of pop, very large navel oranges and dog toys. Their border collie that shared my name was coming with us.

I picked up the incredibly heavy picnic basket to carry it down to the car. My aunt said, "Wait!" and went out of the room and came back with a urinal that she put in a shopping bag and added to the loaded picnic basket. "We might need this," she said. She wasn't a person you questioned.

I loaded my uncle's walker, my father's walker and the picnic basket into the trunk of the rented car and then spread out a blanket for the dog and I got everyone seated. My aunt directed me to a park where she thought we could get almost to the beach. She wouldn't let me use the GPS because she knew a better route. It was November, however, and direct beach access was blocked.

We went to the regular parking lot and I unloaded the two walkers and picnic basket and we began the trek to the beach on the wooden boardwalk. My aunt and uncle zoomed out ahead of us and my father and I puttered along. We reached the end of one boardwalk and had to cross a road to get to the one going down to the beach and my father said, "I have to go to the bathroom."

I said, "I have a urinal."

He said, "How thoughtful." Then he added, "Where should I go?"

I said, "I'll block you. It's November. There is no one else around."

I stood in front of him while he slowly did what he needed to do. He then emptied the urinal and put it back in the shopping bag and handed it back to me. At that moment, my aunt appeared, out of breath, shouting, "Quick, quick, give me the urinal." It was like the Olympic relay as I passed the urinal in its damp shopping bag to her and she ran off.

My father and I continued our way to the beach. At the end of the boardwalk was a barrier that my uncle was holding onto. My father joined him. They watched my aunt throw a ball for the dog over and over again. I looked around thinking, "Where are we going to picnic?" There was a gale force wind and both men were afraid to let go of the barrier. Then it started to rain. My aunt finally arrived back and announced, "I guess we better go back and eat in the car."

We trudged back, and had our picnic with a wet dog in the car. There is something about sandwiches without crusts eaten on china plates while the windows steam up. Even the pop tastes good.

My father died on June 12th 2012. His funeral was packed. He had touched the lives of many people in the years he lived in Sault Ste. Marie. My aunt with her dog Sally came along with her three sons. They persuaded her not to bring the dog to the funeral.

The last weekend I had spent with him was in May. My sister who lived in Sault Ste. Marie, Michigan called o a Saturday and suggested I bring Dad over so we could play cards. Her oldest daughter was visiting so we had enough for a game. My father couldn't remember my name but could still play bridge. It took forever for him to get ready. He gave me his passport then spent 20 minutes looking for it while I was visiting another resident. We got to the car, then he had to return for the bathroom. "You never know how long the lineup will be at the bridge," he said on his return.

Eventually I said we had to go. The traffic was light and we got to my sister's in record time. We started to play. My niece was going through a difficult time and kept leaving the table to have a cry or get some coffee. My father and I could tell she really didn't want to play. At one point she threw her cards on the table, got up and left the room. My father who was not too sure what was happening, used a phrase that he would say to my mother when one of us got into trouble. He turned to me and said, "It's just a phase, you know."

In 2019 Tim and I were awarded the Meritorious Service Cross (civil). The award "recognizes great Canadians for exceptional deeds accomplished over a limited period of time that bring honour to our country. They honour achievements in both military and civil divisions." We spent 10 years raising funds for the Nichola Goddard Foundation. The main project was called Light Up Papua New Guinea and it installed solar lights in first aid clinics in remote areas of Papua New Guinea. There are endowed scholarships in Nichola's name at the University of Calgary and the University of Prince Edward Island. We hosted fundraisers for a decade and managed to donate about half a million dollars.

Tim and I were honoured by the award. If Nichola hadn't been killed, we would never have thought of the project. After ten years, we wanted to pass the torch. In discussion with Victoria and Kate, we soon realized that they both felt it was time to let it go. Kate found True Patriot Love, who quickly created a Captain Nichola Goddard Fund within their organization. It is used primarily to fund projects linked with women and the military.

The project in Papua New Guinea ended when we managed to bring light to over a million people in remote parts of PNG. After almost ten years, people were now able to buy their own solar lights.

503-97 Queen Street, Charlottetown

After much discussion and angst on Tim's part, we have moved into an apartment in downtown Charlottetown, within walking distance of many things. We still have a storage locker containing seasonal items and a number of art pieces and a few more boxes of books. When we first moved, we had two lockers but have now whittled it down to one. Victoria lives about 40 minutes away on 12.5 acres. She has given Tim 5 acres to play with and develop into Grandview Gardens. He's out there most days when the weather is nice, weeding and planting.

We have decided to build an addition onto Victoria's house so that Tim and I have a place to go when it is hot and humid here in town and the downtown area is crawling with tourists. Tim has a shed in his garden, complete with a ¾ bed which is big enough for him and his dog. The outhouse is a good 25 metres from the shed.

Tim has offered to turf the dog but I am holding out for the extension. The sales of Victoria's books has meant that the architect has also designed a conservatory and a library for ~~her~~ our use. It will also mean that when she travels, Tim and I will be able to look after her animals in relative comfort.

Kate is busy on the West Coast, helping start-up companies figure out their legal situation. She has a gorgeous house on the Sunshine Coast with lots of room so when the weather gets bad here, we know where to go.

I spend time playing bridge, cutting grass for Victoria and Tim and working on biographies of people who are interested in sharing their past. I am always on a lookout for a good story.

No one could have predicted my life, but certainly my parents prepared me for it by giving me the skills to cope with situations and places that were completely out of my comfort zone. My husband supported the choices and grew to love the zaniness of my life and the people that I met. Even now, when he comes in after a day in the garden, he expects a story of some kind or at least an anecdote about some idiot I came across in the course of my day.

This is my opus, my final collection.

O Lord, support us all the day long, until the shadows lengthen, and the evening comes, and the busy world is hushed, and the fever of life is over, and our work is done. Then, Lord, in thy mercy, grant us a safe lodging, a holy rest, and peace at the last.

Amen.

—John Henry Newman

About the Author

I was born in England and immigrated to Canada when I was 6 months old. I grew up in Sault Ste Marie, Ontario and after graduating from Trent University, joined CUSO, and taught In Papua New Guinea for almost 10 years. I married there and Nichola, our oldest daughter was almost 4 years old when we left, her sister Victoria was one year old. I worked in many isolated indigenous communities in northern Canada including Black Lake and La Ronge, Saskatchewan; Pangnirtung, Nunavut: and Norman Wells, NWT. Our third daughter, Kate, was born in Saskatoon while my husband was completing his MEd. In southern Canada, I was able to complete my BEd degree at the University of Saskatchewan, and eventually, my MA from the University of Calgary.

As an educator, I have been fortunate to find work wherever my husband's university career has taken him. Jobs have included working on a Cree immersion project for Onion Lake, Saskatchewan; writing news articles for The Northerner, a community based newspaper in La Ronge; teaching in the "Max" (the federal penitentiary) in Edmonton; developing correspondence material for the Nova Scotia Department of Education; teaching junior high in Calgary; and working as an education specialist for the Atlantic Veterinary College in Charlotte-town, Prince Edward Island.

I have also written a book about the life and military career of my daughter Captain Nichola Goddard, *Canada's Daughter*.

www.ingramcontent.com/pod-product-compliance
Lightning Source LLC
Chambersburg PA
CBHW031508120626
46545CB00005B/1794